Born to Heal

Unleash the Supernatural Lifestyle

Jesus Lives in You

Andy Hayner

ISBN-13: 978-1518731723

ISBN-10:1518731724

DEDICATION

To the Lord Jesus Christ,
May You receive the reward of Your suffering
as your saints rise up to release the victory
You purchased through the stripes
on your own back at the whipping post.

The Lamb is worthy!

DISCLAIMER

This is a book on Divine Healing through the power of Jesus Christ.
This book is not intended to give any medical advice.
If, as you are growing in your implementation of the principles contained in
this book you feel the need for medical advice
for yourself or those under your care,
go see a doctor.

CONTENTS

LIST OF FREQUENTLY ASKED QUESTIONS

i

ACKNOWLEDGMENTS

This book could not have been written without the love, prayers, and faithfulness of my family, especially my wife and best friend, Tina. I love you all so much!

I also want to thank my Full Speed Partners, who generously support my ministry and make it possible for me to continue to go to the highways and bi-ways to mobilize believers to walk in the fullness of Jesus Christ worldwide. Your prayers, encouragement, and generosity are touching thousands of lives for eternity! May God bless you.

Lastly, I want to say thank you to Curry Blake and the JGLM family. Thank you for your friendship, encouragement, and partnership in the gospel. When you find a group of people who are laying their lives down to live out the truth and are willing to work through problems with you, you've found something good. You guys are all such a blessing!.

Introduction

God is raising up a worldwide army that is rallying together for a simple reason— that the Lamb of God receive the reward for which He suffered in the lives of every single person. They are discovering that the gospel is more than a message to get us into heaven after we die. It's a message to make us sons and daughters of God now. It's the amazing message that Jesus Christ comes to live inside of us to empower us to walk in His fullness now— and forever! The life that Jesus Christ lives is still just as amazing, and no less compassionate now than when He lived on earth in only one body 2,000 years ago.

But this is not just about healing the sick. This book is a solid reminder to each of us who follow of Jesus Christ that Jesus is really who He said He is, and He that He has not changed anything— except His location. Now He lives *inside* of those who truly believe in Him to empower them. As we develop a lifestyle that comes from wonderful new reality, we will find that the life Jesus Christ has put inside of us is still filled with compassion and able to heal the sick today!

Jesus said, *"Truly, truly, I say to you,* **whoever** *believes in me will also do the works that I do; and greater works than these will he do, because I am going to the Father.* **Whatever** *you ask in my name, this I will do, that the Father may be glorified in the Son. If you ask me* **anything** *in my name, I will do it."* (John 14:12-14) This is Jesus' doctrinal statement concerning every believer. If you believe differently about yourself than Jesus, in these pages you will find ample reasons to put your doubts aside. Shouldn't we be renewing our mind to the mind of Christ?

When the church realizes that she is not without power against sickness and disease, she will arise out of her subdued apathy. It starts by believing the gospel above your experience and above your circumstances.

The message that the Christian believer can minister healing because Jesus Christ is living inside you is revolutionary for many. But the message that every believer has been given the resources to heal anything, anywhere, and anytime through the finished work of Jesus Christ unleashes believers to walk in the fullness of Jesus Christ like nothing else. This is a key missing component of the message Jesus originally entrusted to the apostles, the same message that "turned the world upside down", that is being restored to the church in our day.

This book is written to mobilize believers to overcome every hurdle that is trying to keep you from entering into the full expression of this amazing life that Jesus has purchased for us. Some of these barriers are questions about God's will regarding sickness, like "what about Timothy's stomach" or "what about Paul's thorn". Others are dealing with their own experience— "why am I not healed yet?" or "why am I not seeing more miracles in my ministry?" Still others have never had the benefit of personal mentoring from someone who can give them practical guidance and encouragement to adopt the sort of lifestyle that "fits the Christ who lives inside of them". Whatever challenges you are facing, I believe you will find Biblical and practical help in the pages of this book.

Healing the sick isn't reserved for superstars. It's part of a normal lifestyle intended for any believer. It's the bi-product of a believer who has discovered that Jesus Christ has given us the right to use His authority and power. Jesus paid the price for us to be reconciled to the Father and to walk as true sons and daughters of God, just like Jesus.

The Word of God says, "*But he who is joined to the Lord becomes* **one spirit with him.**"(1 Corinthians 6:17) Believer. Jesus Christ has given you what it takes to set the captives free! You are joint heirs with Jesus (see Romans 8:16). What Jesus has, we as believers have. Learning how to live in His fullness is our destiny, our calling. Nations are waiting. Destinies are at stake!

I offer this book as an encouragement to those who are courageous enough to believe that Jesus Christ wants to work through you to set the captives free and to liberate those oppressed with all kinds of sickness, pain, disease, and even birth defects. May God richly bless you, my brother and sisters, so that those who are still suffering in the grips of satan may be set free to the glory and praise of Jesus Christ! We are what the whole earth has been waiting for with eager expectation. *"For the creation waits with eager longing for the revealing of the sons of God".* (Romans 8:19) God has done what it takes to make you a son. He's waiting on us to wake up to the reality that we are the solution to the problem!

CHAPTER 1

DOES GOD STILL HEAL
SUPERNATURALLY TODAY?

A couple of years ago, I was invited by a pastor to come and pray for a young man, Spencer, in his town that had been run over by a tractor. He was sitting on the wheel cover and came off of it only to wind up with his middle underneath the tractor tire. Spenser had five major bone shattered— both hips, the pelvis bones, and two lower vertebrae.

The pastor had arranged for me to come over to the house for prayer, so we pulled up to farm house about 10am. We walked into the living room, where Spenser's hospital bed and wheel chair had taken over the center of the room.

The entire family had gathered to greet us and watch— dad, mom, brother, sister, and girlfriend. Just in case that wasn't enough, Spenser's grandmother pulled into the drive just as we began to introduce ourselves to one another.

As we introduced ourselves, we learned that Spenser was unable to move the lower half of his body except by pulling his legs around with his own hands and arms. This was very difficult and painful. He had numbness, shooting pain, and constant dull pain. There was a great deal of uncertainty if Spenser would ever walk again, or whether he would be in pain for the rest of his life. The concern and weariness that hung in the air was even more palpable than the smell of urine that hung in the air because of the catheter bag hanging on a hook on the side of Spenser's bed.

As Spenser's grandmother entered the room, she shook my hand, and said ever so sweetly, "It's so nice of you come here and pray." But something in her tone of voice and demeanor made me feel like she was assuming that nothing special was going to happen. In her mind, we were just there to show support for the family. I felt it was important for me to rise above that expectation so I spoke up, "I'm glad to be here, but my job isn't to just show support for your family. My job is to freak Spencer's doctors out and get Spenser healed."

With that, I explained a little more about what Jesus has done to accomplish our healing. Then I laid my hands on Spenser's hips and believed God for his healing. After a few minutes, I asked Spenser to check out his mobility and tell me what he noticed. He immediately pulled his legs up to a forty-five degree angle on his bed without using his hands or arms, prompting several of Spenser's family members to gasp and then begin to cry. I invited my pastor friend, his wife, and my son to also lay hands on Spenser, which took less than ten minutes.

When they were finished I asked Spenser, "Are you ready?" He looked at me and said, "Ready for what?" I said, "To get out of that bed and walk!" He immediately began to move on his bed, pulling his torso upright with an overhanging "pull up bar", and then he swung his legs off the side of the bed without using his hands or arms. I asked, "How are you feeling?" Spenser responded with a smile, "I feel good." "Any pain?" I asked. He said, "No. I'm feeling good."

His mother had brought over a four pronged walker that Spenser had been unable to use for anything more than bracing to assist maneuvering himself into a wheelchair. With the walker positioned in front of him, Spenser stood straight up on his feet beside the bed without even touching the walker. So I pulled the walker out of his way so that Spenser could walk. He took three steps away from the bed completely unassisted as his family cried, cheered, and clapped! Spenser then returned to his bed, and said, "I don't have any pain, but I still feel a little wobbly." So Spenser continued sitting perfectly upright with his legs hanging over the bed as we talked with the family.

At this point, I shared with the whole family, "It's obvious to see from your reaction that God has done a real miracle here today. I'm not sure where each of you are in your personal faith, but I would say this would be a good time for each of us to get right with God. He's so good. He sent Jesus to be our Savior and Lord, by living for us a perfect life, dying for our sin, and rising from the dead. He's alive and real. He loves you and wants to forgive you and make your life brand new." At that point, I led everyone in the room to call on Jesus for salvation.

The next day I received an update from the pastor. He had seen someone who was with us at Spenser's home in his neighborhood that morning. He asked them, "So how was Spenser after we left?" "Guess what they said," the pastor said to me. I could tell from the pastor's tone of voice, it must be good. He went on to say, "They told me that Spenser went out riding his Gator (like a four wheeler designed like a flatbed truck) around the farm for *three hours that afternoon* with absolutely no pain!" Praise Jesus!

WHY CHRISTIANS DON'T ALWAYS HEAL

If Jesus Christ lives inside of us, why wouldn't we expect Him to do miracles through us? Has He lost His power? Has He lost His compassion? Has He changed? Does the world no longer need witnesses of Jesus Christ who are clothed with the power of the Holy Spirit? Would genuine miracles somehow undermine the message of a completed Bible, or could they serve the same function as they did with the first apostles… as signs pointing to the true Word? When Christians exhibit the character and power of God, doesn't this affirm the authority of the Word of God?

Many Bible believing Christians have a great deal of confusion surrounding the ministry of healing. Many people started out believing, but then someone they prayed for didn't get healed and they got confused. They allowed their confusion to hinder their faith. Jesus Christ is not at all confused about healing the sick. Many ministers are practicing things regarding healing that Jesus nor the apostles ever did or ever taught. Our problem is that we believe so many things about sickness that Jesus Christ and the apostles didn't. We need our mind renewed.

For the past few years, I have traveled to many different churches and several different continents to mobilize believers to walk in the power of Jesus Christ. I find that the church has been very well taught on "why people don't get healed", "why God doesn't always heal", "10 things that block miracles" and things like this. We are saturated with this kind of "theology." Is it any wonder the church is walking in so little of Jesus' power? Did Jesus believe these kinds of things? When Jesus walked up to someone who needed a miracle, did he wonder if God wanted them healed? Did Jesus say, "I'm sorry, I've been writing this book about 10 things that block miracles and you have 3 of them. So I can't help you today. Sorry?" Christ had none of these things in His belief system. They weren't in His mind, then or now! We need to live "by the faith of the Son of God" (Gal. 2:20 KJV) and renew our minds to the mind of Christ. If Jesus didn't believe sickness was God's will, should we? Shouldn't we walk according to the mind of Christ?

Despite the fact that the Bible is filled with examples and promises regarding God's will to heal the sick by His grace and power, many evangelical Christians have doubts about whether God will still heal today. They gladly receive prayer to "guide the doctor's hands" and encouragement that "God is in control" (as if God wants them sick for a higher purpose). Some churches are even quick to organize practical support for meals, rides, and laundry for those who are suffering illness (which is a wonderful thing when it's necessary). But some Christians recoil with suspicion if a congregant on the "sick list" calls the church and says, "You can tell everyone that had planned to help me with meals that I'm fine now. This lady came over to my house, laid hands on me, and all the sickness and pain are completely gone! I'm healed! It was a miracle!"

Believe it or not, some pastors, rather than rejoicing with praise, would feel threatened if someone stood up during the announcements to share the testimony of a healing miracle such as this at their church. If someone begins to teach members of the church how to minister healing that gets results, many pastors get downright agitated. Why is this?

For much of my Christian life, I too was very skeptical of any Christian who claimed that God did a miracle through them. I had seen many "miracle working ministers" exposed for their greed, immorality, and deceit by the news programs. I had also seen the moral and intellectual disgust of men that I respected as they strained out the theological and personal flaws of these supposed "men of God". More than this, I saw my own family members and friends continue to suffer from various diseases and maladies despite the earnest prayers for healing by many Christians.

What could make someone as skeptical as I once was, have the audacity to write a book to challenge and encourage the church to believe God for the supernatural healing of every sickness, disease, defect, and pain? The simple answer is that **the Word of God changed my mind.**. As I changed my mind to believe what God's Word says about healing, I began to see the power of God operate through me to heal people. In fact, in the past few years I have seen thousands of miraculous healings of almost every affliction known to mankind— leukemia, C.O.P.D., autism, cerebral palsy, diabetes, blindness, deafness, cancer, broken bones, and more— all healed by the power of Jesus Christ alone.

Before you get too impressed with me (or skeptical), as I've traveled throughout the USA and around the world I've trained hundreds of other believers who are now seeing God heal the sick through them. I'm convinced that God will do His mighty works through *any believer*. You may have questions or doubts about this, but you'll need to take it up with Jesus. Because Jesus Christ Himself believes He can heal the sick through any believer too! Jesus said, "*Truly, truly, I say to you,* **whoever believes in Me** *will also do the works that I do; and greater works than these will he do, because I am going to the Father.*" (John 14:12) Whether or not you have ever experienced healing up to this point in your life, you must understand that Jesus Christ believes He can heal the sick through "*whoever believes"* in Him. But note this well, *believing comes before the healing.*

I was recently given an electric guitar and amplifier as a gift from my family. One afternoon I went to play it but could not get any sound to come out. I jiggled all the cords and turned the knobs for twenty minutes, but couldn't make it work. I knew there was plenty of electricity available from the outlet because I could see it working in my computer and my printer. But believing in the availability of electricity wasn't helping my guitar! I was just about to start to look for my receipt, convinced that something was broken, when I realized that there was a switch on my extension cord that had flipped to the off position. With one simple flip, the "off switch" became an "on switch" and the power began to flow.

In the same way, dear Christian, you may see the power and grace of God working all around you— in creation, in your salvation, in your marriage, in

His Word— but as you align yourself with the Word of God regarding healing, you will see the power of God begin to flow in this area as well. As your mind is renewed to His Word, His power will flow freely through you. Meanwhile, rest assured, God's power and grace is available for healing all sickness, disease, and defect.

CHAPTER 2

FIXING OUR EYES

Recently, I was over at a friend's house to lead a discipleship class. At a certain point, I had the group pair up for some exercises, and it happened that I was left without a partner. Since I was already very familiar with this particular skill, I wondered over to play legos with one of the children.

This young girl had brought over a great big plastic tub filled with legos, which were now conveniently dumped in a pile in the corner of the room. She was diligently building a city of some sort, and making some recognizable progress. As we chatted, I decided to "help" and picked up a couple of pieces that I recognized and made a small car. I rolled it across the floor to the young girl and said, "Look! I made a car." She grabbed it and said, "It's not right" and started to take it apart. She said, "That's not how those pieces work in this set."

For most Christians, the Bible is a very confusing book. It's like trying to make sense of a pile of legos. Every verse of Scripture is like a different lego piece. We try to gain a sense orientation making some connections that seem to make sense to us. We construct our little "doctrines" that seem to hold together and roll well enough. The problem is that we've left a lot of lego pieces out, and there seems to be so many different possible ways to put them together.

Jesus, not our theological tradition or our personal experience, is the definitive and authoritative revelation of God regarding healing the sick. In contrast, most clergy have been trained to develop theology by picking verses out the Bible like pulling lego pieces out of a set and arranging them together in an organized system. In the process sometimes they end up putting the lego pieces together to form a construction that looks *nothing like the picture on the cover of the box*. As I said in my previous book, **Immersed into God**, "Bible verses are like puzzle pieces. *Jesus Christ is the picture on the* *box*. So if we put our Bible verses together in a way that looks different than the character, life, and teachings of Jesus Christ, then we need to start over."

Jesus Christ is perfect theology. Just in case we don't understand the words, God gave us a picture! Jesus Christ is the Word made flesh. It is very easy to put the pieces together wrong, so we need to keep checking with the picture that God gave us of Himself. Jesus Christ is a portrait of the invisible God. He is the perfect revelation of God's will and ways regarding love, salvation, and yes… healing. He is the absolute revelation of the Father, which is why Jesus could say, *"Whoever has seen me has seen the Father."* (John 14:9)

It's important to keep in mind, that we do not see God revealing Himself as "our Father in heaven" until Jesus Christ. Many Bible believing Christians are confused because they do not understand the significant shift that has taken place with the coming of Jesus Christ and the establishing of the New Covenant.

For example, many Christians have read the book of Job and noticed that although God was not directly responsible for Job's affliction (Satan was the one afflicting Job), God was very aware of the sickness and pain that Satan was inflicting upon him. When they find themselves battling with a prolonged disease, pain, or sickness they associate themselves with Job, saying, "Well, maybe I'm just like Job."

Although this is certainly Biblical, when you hold this line of reasoning up to the light of Jesus Christ, the "I'm just like Job" mindset unravels. Here's why— the book of Job was in Jesus' Bible too, right? Yet do we ever see Jesus Christ being asked to heal someone only to send them away, saying, "I wish I could heal you, but you are just like Job. God wants you to stay sick a while longer so that He can be glorified as Satan afflicts you?" Did Jesus ever do anything like this? No, He never did. Jesus' presence on the earth brought far more to the table than Job or anyone else in the Old Testament period had ever known. Indeed, since Jesus Christ, "The Kingdom of Heaven is at hand!"

For from his fullness we have all received, grace upon grace. For the law was given through Moses; grace and truth came through Jesus Christ. (John 1:16-17)

With Jesus, there is a significant shift in the way God relates to us. Before Jesus Christ, God was unable to fully reveal or express Himself in the relationship that He created us to enjoy. (see Heb. 1:1-2) Imagine a man who is both a father and judge. If this man's child is arrested and is brought before him to stand trial, the father must act as a judge towards his child. The father is not free to begin each day in court by coming down from his bench and giving his son a big hug and a reassuring pep talk. The father may even have to sentence his son to jail if justice requires it. However, after the trial has concluded and justice is served, the judge can now take off his robe and relate to his child as a father.

This is exactly what is happening in Jesus Christ. Before Christ, although God wanted to restore us into right relationship with Him as sons and daughters, justice had not yet been served. God established a covenant with one nation, Israel, and gave promises and laws to them specifically, in order to bring about His salvation through Jesus Christ. Prior to this, God could not treat us as sons and daughters. Through Jesus Christ, God is able close the case against humanity through the cross. Justice has been served at the cross. The Father has revealed His true nature in Jesus Christ so that He could reestablish His predestined way of relating towards us— namely, as sons of God.

ACCORDING TO CHRIST?

*See to it that no one takes you captive by philosophy and empty deceit, according to human tradition, according to the elemental spirits of the world, and not **according to Christ.*** Col 2:8

Jesus Christ is not only the perfect revelation of the Father. He is also the perfect revelation of the Christian life. The Christian life is *"no longer I who live, but Christ who lives in me"* (Gal. 2:20). In the church, there may many different lifestyles, but *"whoever says he abides in Him ought to walk in the same way in which He walked.*" (1 Jn. 2:6) What does Jesus' walk show us about how we should walk healing the sick? Jesus Christ hasn't changed His lifestyle. He moved into you to change your lifestyle!

Among the various denominations, there may be a number of mindsets about healing sickness and disease, but Jesus Christ has only one mindset. His mindset is the only one that is right and the only one that matters! We have been given the "mind of Christ" (1 Cor. 2:6), but we will only experience the power of Jesus Christ as we adopt His mindset. We have a very simple grid to evaluate every teaching and tradition— is this what Jesus believed, taught, and demonstrated? The foundation of the Christian faith is not our theological tradition or denominational teaching. Our foundation must be Jesus Christ Himself. If what we are believing didn't come from Him, then it'd be a good idea to give it up.

This is especially important when it comes to the subject of sickness and healing. Whatever we may believe about God's will regarding sickness and healing, we must hold this up beside Jesus Christ to see whether it looks like what the Father has revealed about Himself in Christ.

Let's practice this with some beliefs that are popularly held by the church today. For example, for many years I was taught a view of God's sovereignty that led to the belief that if someone is sick, it's because it is the "sovereign will of God" for them to be so, usually to accomplish God's higher purpose, perhaps to teach them something or draw them closer to Himself. Even now, I could string together several Bible verses to make a convincing argument for this teaching.

But let's hold this up next to Jesus Christ, God's own personal revelation of Himself. What do we see in Him? Do we see Jesus Christ making people sick to teach them a lesson? No! Do we see Jesus leaving people sick to develop their character or to draw them closer to Himself? Of course not. Do we see Jesus Christ on the hillsides and seashores of Palestine, with the multitudes carrying their sick and injured to Him, only to have Him say, "Beloved, be encouraged. You are only sick because your heavenly Father wants to use this in your life for your greater good and His glory. Now, go home in peace." On the contrary, we see that Jesus continually "healed all who were sick." (Matt. 8:16) Whatever we may believe about the doctrine of God's sovereignty, any view of His sovereignty that would make God "pro-sickness" instead of "pro-healing" is a terrible misunderstanding of the Word of God.

WHOEVER, WHENEVER, FROM WHATEVER

Jesus was **always** willing to heal **whoever** needed healing **whenever** they came to Him. Whenever Jesus came to town, *"great crowds came to him, bringing with them the lame, the blind, the crippled, the mute, and many others, and they put them at his feet, and **He healed them**."* (Matt. 15:30) When Jesus left town, *"many followed him, and **He healed them all**."* (Matt. 12:15)

Through Jesus Christ, God demonstrated that He's not the one making people sick or leaving people sick. At every turn, Jesus Christ was healing people. The apostle Peter affirms this when He says, "God anointed Jesus of Nazareth with the Holy Spirit and with power. He went about doing good and *healing all who were oppressed by the devil*, for God was with him."(Act 10:37-38) Jesus never treated sickness or disease as the work or will of His Father. He always treated sickness and disease as a work of the enemy that God wanted removed by the power and authority of the Kingdom of God.

Soon after I began to discover these truths, I remember an incident in which I was at a church that had a special ministry time that was opened up for those in attendance at the meeting. There was one man who said that he had suffered pain in his feet and legs for a number of years and wanted to be healed. There was an older gentleman near me who heard the request and said, "Sure, we'll pray for you and see what God will do." I responded, "No we won't." They both looked at me like I was crazy. I continued by saying, "We don't have to pray to see what God will do. We have to study the Word. Jesus showed us that He heals all who have need of healing and come to Him. The Word says that believers will lay hands on the sick and they will be healed. (Mark:16:18) Jesus commands His disciples to heal the sick. (Mt. 10:7-8) We already know what God will do. Now, let's pray so that God can do what He does!" As we took a firm stand upon the revealed will of God, healing was released and we "saw what God does."

Jesus' ministry was a continual demonstration of *the will of the Father regarding healing.*

*"I seek not my own will but **the will of Him who sent me.**"* (John 5:30)

*"For I have come down from heaven, not to do my own will but **the will of Him who sent me.**"* (John 6:38)

In Christ, we see clearly that the Father is **always** willing to heal **whoever** needs healing **whenever** they come to Him. Indeed, *"Behold, now is the favorable time; behold, now is the day of salvation."* (2 Cor. 6:2) Everything included in salvation, according to the Scriptures, is available NOW. Jesus is able to deliver us from evil in all its various forms— sin, guilt, and sickness. This is good news indeed! God is not the cause of prolonging sickness or delaying healing.

If a Christian sins, is that God's will? Of course not. You'd be wrong to tell them, "It's not always God's will to give you victory over sin" simply because they fell into temptation. If a born-again-believer is struggling to overcome an addiction, it's not because they need God to give them something that they don't yet have. Is it? They just need to learn to walk in all that they have received in Christ. They need to be transformed in their mind until their lifestyle is transformed to become what God put inside them. So we know that we shouldn't look at our lives to determine whether it is God's will for us to walk in victory. We look at the Word until our lives look like the Word. We should take this approach for healing as well as holiness. Jesus Christ has provided us victory over evil, the devil and all His works, which includes sickness as well as sin.

IS IT GOD'S TIMING OR OUR SLOWNESS?

Another thing we often hear Christians say is, "I know God wants you to be healed, but it may not be His perfect timing." While this may sound true and even fit with our personal experience, let's not be like those who live according to the "way that *seems right* to a man" because "its end is the way to death." (Prov. 14:12) Instead, let us *"fix our eyes upon Jesus, the author and finisher of our faith."* (Heb. 12:1)

What do we see in Jesus? Does He embrace the "God has a certain time appointed for your healing, so I'm afraid you'll have to wait until next Thursday" approach to sickness? Jesus was constantly being approached spontaneously by people for physical healing. Do we ever see Jesus Christ say, "I'm sorry. It's not God's timing for your healing just yet. I'll see you again next Passover?" Thankfully we see no such thing.

There are only two incidents in the life of Jesus Christ that come anywhere close to possible exceptions that support the "God's perfect timing" mindset regarding healing. The first is when Jesus initially declined to heal a gentile woman's daughter. However, this had nothing to do with God's timing for the girl. It was due to the fact that Jesus was sent first to Israel as their Messiah, and the time to release the blessings of the Kingdom to the Gentiles had not yet come. Since the establishing of the New Covenant however, the children's bread— physical healing— is available to all, both Jew and Gentile. Furthermore, even in this instance, Jesus ended up healing the gentile woman's daughter even though she had no covenant to support a relationship with God.

The other instance that is sometimes raised to support the "all in God's perfect timing" mindset is Jesus refusing to come immediately when He received word that Lazarus was sick. On the surface, this instance may seem to lend some credibility that God may delay healing. However, a little careful reading shows us that this isn't the case at all. What does the passage actually say? Let's read it.

> *It was Mary who anointed the Lord with ointment and wiped his feet with her hair, whose brother Lazarus was ill. So the sisters sent to him, saying, "Lord, he whom you love is ill." But* **when Jesus heard it he said, "This illness does not lead to death. It is for the glory of God, so that the Son of God may be glorified through it."** *Now Jesus loved Martha and her sister and Lazarus. So,* **when he heard that**

> ***Lazarus was ill, he stayed two days longer*** *in the place where he was. Then after this he said to the disciples, "Let us go to Judea again." …After saying these things, he (Jesus) said to them, "Our friend Lazarus has fallen asleep, but I go to awaken him." The disciples said to him, "Lord, if he has fallen asleep, he will recover." Now Jesus had spoken of his death, but they thought that he meant taking rest in sleep. Then Jesus told them plainly,* **"Lazarus has died, and for your sake I am glad that I was not there, so that you may believe.** *But let us go to him."… So Thomas, called the Twin, said to his fellow disciples, "Let us also go, that we may die with him." Now* **when Jesus came, he found that Lazarus had already been in the tomb four days.** (John 11:2-14)

In case you missed it, here's how the events unfolded. Mary and Martha sent for Jesus, who had just left from Jerusalem, because their brother Lazarus was ill. By the time Jesus received the message that Lazarus was ill He knew by the Holy Spirit that Lazarus had already died. How do I know this? Because, Jesus only waited around for **two days** after receiving the news of Lazarus's illness, but when He arrived at Lazarus' tomb, Lazarus had already been dead **four days**. Lazarus must have died shortly after the messenger was dispatched, which would mean that he was already dead when Jesus was told he was ill.

This makes it clear that Jesus wasn't delaying his departure because God was somehow "getting more glory" from Lazarus remaining sick. Jesus remained where He was because Lazarus was already dead by the time Jesus received news of Lazarus's illness. So rather than returning quickly, Jesus waited around so that Lazarus could get *extremely dead*— so dead that no one would be able to deny the glory of God as it was manifested by Jesus Christ raising Lazarus from death. So the next time someone tries to pull this verse out of context to tell you that sicknesses are for the "glory of God", you can tell them that the only way God displays His glory regarding sickness is to heal it or raise someone from the dead. God does **not** display His glory by leaving people sick.

IS GOD PLAYING "DUCK, DUCK, GOOSE" or "EENIE, MEENIE, MINY, MOE"?

There is a popular mindset along these lines that remains in the church—that although God has the power to heal those who are sick, He is deciding on a case by case basis whether He wants to heal or not. "I know God can heal me," the theory goes, "Whether He wants to or not is up to Him." As believers in Christ, we love and trust God regardless of whatever attacks we may endure from Satan. However, it's very discouraging indeed to believe that God is able to heal but has decided to leave you or your loved one miserable, oppressed, and excluded.

Is this how the Father was manifest in Jesus Christ, deciding on a case by case basis? When entire villages brought their sick and injured for Jesus to heal, do we see Jesus picking and choosing some to heal and others to leave in misery?

*That evening they brought to him many who were oppressed by demons, and he cast out the spirits with a word and **healed all who were sick**.* (Mat 8:16)

*Jesus, aware of this, withdrew from there. And **many followed him, and he healed them all.*** (Mat 12:15)

*But when the crowds heard it, they followed him on foot from the towns. When he went ashore he saw **a great crowd**, and **he had compassion on them and healed their sick.*** (Matt. 14:13-14)

Thankfully, we don't see Jesus playing "Duck, Duck, Goose" when it comes to healing, randomly excluding people who came for healing, leaving them passed over to remain in their bondage. So we can confidently say that God is not selective or exclusive when it comes to healing. In fact, Jesus seemed more upset when people refused to come to Him for healing, such as when His hometown took offense at Him.(Mark 6:1-5) How could Jesus command His disciples to "heal the sick" (Mt. 10:8) with no exceptions whatsoever unless God was also willing to heal the sick with no exceptions? If one of Jesus' disciples (which would include us) sees someone who is sick (any and all sicknesses) we are commanded to minister healing by the power of the Kingdom, which is very good news for us and them.

The only incident in the life of Jesus Christ that is sometimes used to support the idea that God is passing those who are sick to select one lucky person for the "miracle of the day" is this:

After this there was a feast of the Jews, and Jesus went up to Jerusalem. Now there is in Jerusalem by the Sheep Gate a pool, in Aramaic called Bethesda, which has five roofed colonnades. In these lay a multitude of invalids—blind, lame, and paralyzed. One man was there who had been an invalid for thirty-eight years. When **Jesus saw him** *lying there and knew that he had already been there a long time, he said to him, "Do you want to be healed?" The sick man answered him, "Sir, I have no one to put me into the pool when the water is stirred up, and while I am going another steps down before me." Jesus said to him, "Get up, take up your bed, and walk." And at once the man was healed, and he took up his bed and walked. Now that day was the Sabbath. So the Jews said to the man who had been healed, "It is the Sabbath, and it is not lawful for you to take up your bed." But he answered them, "The man who healed me, that man said to me, 'Take up your bed, and walk.'" They asked him, "Who is the man who said to you, 'Take up your bed and walk'?" Now the man who had been healed did not know who it was,* **for Jesus had withdrawn, as there was a crowd in the place.** *Afterward Jesus found him in the temple and said to him, "See, you are well! Sin no more, that nothing worse may happen to you."* **The man went away and told the Jews that it was Jesus who had healed him. And this was why the Jews were persecuting Jesus, because he was doing these things on the Sabbath.** (Joh 5:1-16)

What are we to make of Jesus, healing only one man at the Sheep Gate pool where "lay a multitude of invalids"? Jerusalem had become a dangerous place for Jesus. The last time Jesus was there he drove out the money changers and created a huge stir so that even powerful people, such as Nicodemous, a ruler of the Jews, had to wait until the cover of night to go and visit Jesus. The hostility of the environment influenced how Jesus operated and made it difficult for "seekers" to openly investigate Jesus or confess faith in Him.

In this situation, Jesus healed the one man, presumably amongst a multitude who needed healing(but note that this IS an assumption). Jesus healed the man with a "Holy Ghost drive-by" and then slipped away before the man had any idea of who had healed him. Why? Apparently, after healing this one man, the combination between the location, the crowd dynamics, the Sabbath day, and the hostility of the religious rulers of Jerusalem made it impossible for Jesus to spend the entire day healing everyone at the Sheep Gate pool. Jesus wasn't picking and choosing which sick He would heal, and which He would leave in misery. Jesus was avoiding a predictably unstable situation that would have resulted in Him getting cornered by a crowd that could quickly become a violent mob if instigated by the hostile religious rulers or forcing Him to be King if the mob were favorable.

This is further confirmed by recognizing that Jesus had a regular ministry of healing entire villages all throughout Israel. Before Jesus came to town, the villages were filled with people who were diseased, demonized, blind, deaf, lame, and crippled from birth. When He left, everyone was healthy and at peace. He never once singled anyone out to exclude them from healing! Why? Jesus answered this question Himself by saying, "*I only do what I see my Father doing.*" (John 5:19) The Father never excludes anyone from healing, so Jesus was always ready to heal anyone who had any need of healing. He is making God manifest— **always** ready to heal **anyone** who had **any** need for healing!

How many times have you heard people end their prayer for healing with the phrase, "**IF** it be Thy will" as if God's will regarding healing is still in question? In many ways, they are as spiritually confused as Philip, who asked Jesus "*Lord, just show us the Father, and it is enough for us.*" (John 14:8). Even though he had already walked with Jesus throughout His entire ministry. *Jesus replied ""Don't you know me, Philip, even after I have been among you such a long time? Anyone who has seen me has seen the Father. How can you say, 'Show us the Father'?"*

I labor this point because there are so many Christians who have a concept of God that is nowhere close to how God revealed Himself through Jesus Christ. When lives are cut short because of sickness or disease, Christians wonder out loud, "Why did God do this?" thinking that God is the cause of sickness instead of the Healer! When a Christian gets a bad report from the doctor, they turn to God in disillusioned despair instead of confidence and relief that He has already provided Himself as their solution in advance. When a child is born with defect, instead of recognizing these defects as an attack of the enemy and mobilizing the resources of the Kingdom of God to set them free, most believers mistakenly attribute these defects to God's plan and design.

"Have I been with you so long, and you still do not know me?" is a fair question for Jesus to ask not just Phillip, but each of His disciples today. The revelation that Jesus gave Phillip is the very truth we need to take to heart, *"If you had known me, you would have known my Father also. From now on you do know Him and have seen him…Whoever has seen me has seen the Father."* We must see that God has revealed Himself fully and clearly in Jesus Christ as the one whose will is always healing.

*"Truly, truly, I say to you, the Son can do nothing of his own accord, but **only what he sees the Father doing**. For whatever the Father does, that the Son does likewise."* (John 5:19)

"I have manifested Your Name to the people whom you gave me out of the world." (John 17:6)

Judging by the life of Jesus Christ, it is safe to say that He **never** saw the Father making people sick or leaving people sick. Jesus saw the Father healing and showed Him to us by the things He did. Jesus manifested the nature of the Father. He is like a computer monitor live streaming the Father on earth. As we look at Him we see the Father's works. As we hear Jesus, we hear the Father's words. What is it that we see and hear? Our heavenly Father is a healer. He always heals **whoever** is brought to Him **whenever** they come from **whatever** they have been afflicted. That's wonderful news for those of us who have loved ones who need healing!

I remember one lady who asked me to pray for her healing. She had been suffering for years with chronic pain as the result of an automobile accident.

She had also had many people pray for her but had not yet experienced healing. So I laid hands on her and ministered healing. After a short while, I asked her to move around and tell me if she noticed any change. She informed me that she still felt pain as she moved. But then she immediately began to explain to me that she was sure that she would be healed "in God's perfect timing." I stopped her to assure her that, "God's time for your healing was 2,000 years ago when Jesus suffered at the whipping post. Today is the day of salvation! Now is the time!" I laid hands on her and ministered a bit longer and she was completely healed. Had I bought into the 'God's timing' teaching, I would not have had the confidence that allowed me to persist for her healing.

I remember another time that a lady approached me for prayer. She said, "I had an automobile accident many years ago that cause me to have to have my tailbone removed. I have constant pain." So I took her by the hands (note: you DON'T need to touch the place that needs to be healed directly) and said, "In the Name of Jesus, pain go now! Be healed and fully restored." Then I said, "Move around a bit and tell me if you notice any change." When she moved she said, "I still feel a little pain." I laid hands and ministered a couple of more times without the pain leaving completely. Yet I wasn't discouraged or worried. I encouraged her to thank God that He's working and let me know if she needs more prayer.

The next day, I saw her in the hall. She approached me with a big smile and said, "This morning something amazing happened. It *grew back! My tail bone has grown back and I am pain free for the first time in twenty years!*" Praise the Lord! Nothing is impossible with God!

CHAPTER 3

EXERCISING FAITH

IF HEALING IS GOD'S WILL, WHAT'S THE HOLD UP?

One day Jesus was coming down from the Mount of Transfiguration and was met by a man who had brought his son to be set free from a demonic affliction. Although the disciples had not been able to get the boy free, Jesus immediately set the boy free, thus demonstrating it was the will of God for the boy to be healed and free. Note this well—despite the fact that it was God's will to heal the boy, and that the disciples had been given the authority to heal him, the disciples were unable to do so. It was God's will for the boy to be healed and free, but it didn't happen for the disciples! Why?

What if Jesus had delayed his decent from the mountain long enough so that the father decided to return home with his son? Can you imagine the conversation that might have unfolded between the disciples, as they waited at the base of the mountain? I'm sure the disciples would have come up with all kinds of good, Biblical reasons that the boy didn't get healed.

If they were anything like "Christians" today, I can imagine them saying things like:

- Perhaps God is preparing this father for a ministry to other parents with sick children.

- It probably wasn't God's timing.

- I'll bet this boy was under a generational curse. I think his grandfather was a high level Mason.

- I think the father had too much unbelief and had been speaking too many negative confessions over his son.

- God disciplines those He loves, so somebody must be in   trouble or that boy would be healed by now.

There is no end to all the "Biblical" excuses that disciples of Jesus Christ make for people not getting healed. Unfortunately, the need to justify that position with Bible verses often only gets worse when a person has a seminary degree and an official ministry title. All these principles "seem right to a man", right up to the point that Jesus Christ shows up and sets the boy free! Apparently Jesus doesn't buy into all the theology about "why God doesn't always heal" or "Ten ways we block our healing." Jesus shows us that **God's will is always healing, but He accomplishes His healing work through our faith.**

This incident challenges us on a personal level, to grow as disciples of Jesus Christ, because it shows us that the delay to the boy's healing was not the boy, nor the father of the boy, nor was it God! God's will for the boy was healing and freedom. Jesus expected the disciples to be able to set the boy free, and Jesus isn't wrong! Yet the boy had not been healed despite the disciple's best efforts and the father's earnest expectation. What then was the hold up?

> *And I brought him to your disciples, and they could not heal him." And Jesus answered,* **"O faithless and twisted generation,** *how long am I to be with you? How long am I to bear with you? Bring him here to me."… Then the disciples came to Jesus privately and said,* **"Why could we not cast it out?" He said to them, "Because of your little faith.** *For truly, I say to you, if you have faith like a grain of mustard seed, you will say to this mountain, 'Move from here to there,' and it will move, and nothing will be impossible for you."* (Matt. 17:16-20)

Notice, unlike many modern churches, Jesus never blamed a sick person, nor their family members as the cause of the delay for a healing. Nor was God the problem. According to Jesus, the reason for the delay was the disciples themselves. They had twisted thinking that was making their faith ineffective. Jesus isn't blaming the disciples, but He is strongly challenging them to have confidence in God for healing through them. He expects His disciples to be able to set people free. If we are not seeing the results that Jesus expects the Kingdom to produce through His disciples, we must change our expectations and get rid of the twisted thinking that is causing our faith to be ineffective.

"So, if my child isn't healed, it's my fault? Is that what you are saying?" Absolutely not! Your child's afflictions are not your fault, nor are they God's! Rather than pointing the finger, I am pointing you to Jesus Christ as the way forward for you and your child. I want to encourage you to see that it is always God's will to heal. Instead of thinking you are hopeless or powerless in the face of sickness and disease, I want to encourage you with the good news that God wants to empower you and use you to help those who are being oppressed with afflictions.

God wants this revelation to fill our hearts with hope, so that we will rise up and throw off the lies of the devil that give so much place for his destructive power to work in our lives. We can move forward in the confidence that it is Jesus' plan to heal the sick through us. While we should never walk around feeling guilty for people's affliction (after all, it's the devil that is oppressing them, not us!) we must nonetheless accept the responsibility to grow up into the image of Christ, so that Jesus is able to express Himself through us in fullness. As we allow the Word of God to remove the twisted mindsets within us and replace it with the mind of Christ, we will begin to see Christ accomplish His mighty works through us to help those who desperately need His touch.

STEPPING BEYOND YOUR EXPERIENCE

We make a serious mistake if we draw our conclusions about God from our personal experience of life. Jesus called this way of living "walking in darkness." (John 12:46) This is what makes our mindsets "twisted" and keeps God's power from flowing freely through us. For example, you may have had a horrid childhood, but you would be mistaken to think that God loves you less than the child born into a loving Christian home. If you struggle to pay your bills, you would be mistaken to think that God has less favor in His heart towards you than the man who just got a promotion with a nice pay increase.

Jesus said, *"I have come into the world as light."* (John 12:46) Only by looking at Jesus can we see the truth about God, ourselves, and this world. We may have experienced a lot events that made us feel unloved, rejected, worthless, and condemned. But if we want to see how God truly feels about us we must stop "leaning on our own understanding" and look to the cross, where once and for all *"God demonstrates His loves towards us in this— while we were yet sinners, Christ died for us."* (Rom. 5:8) The cross of Jesus Christ, not our circumstances, is the place we must look to see God's love for us.

If you want to see how much God has blessed you, you don't look at your wallet or bank account! You look to the Word of God that declares that in Christ you have already been blessed *"every spiritual blessing in the heavenly places."* (Eph. 1:3) Every blessing heaven has to offer is already yours and constantly at your disposal. But if you continue to believe what your circumstances are telling you is more reliable than what the Word of God says, you may not experience these blessings. Just because there is no water flowing out of the faucet, doesn't mean there is no water available. We need to open the tap and leave the water running!

If we are ever going to become agents of God's healing power, we must decide to believe the Word of God above our own feelings, medical "facts", people who "prayed and nothing happened," and all our denominational traditions.

*See to it that no one takes you captive by philosophy and empty deceit, according to human tradition, according to the elemental principles of the world, and not **according to Christ.*** (Col 2:8)

Only as we fix our eyes upon Jesus Christ, will our twisted mindsets be removed so that we begin to see God clearly. In the same way that we can only know the love and forgiveness of God through Christ on the cross, we must first know the healing of God through Christ at the whipping post. Before we can minister healing and see healing accomplished in the bodies of those who are afflicted, we must first see healing accomplished in the body of Jesus Christ by the stripes He suffered at the whipping post.

THE CROSS AND THE WHIPPING POST

At the cross, Jesus Christ bore our sins and carried them away so that we can go free. The cross reveals the value that God places upon each one of us. What an awesome price He paid for our forgiveness, so that He can restore us to our created destiny.

What He did for our sins at the cross, He did for our diseases, pains, and sicknesses at the whipping post. When Jesus suffered stripes on His back at the whipping post, He purchased healing for our physical bodies so that "*by His stripes we were healed.*" (Is. 53:5) The choice of words in the original languages and the fact that this very passage is quoted in the gospel of Matthew make it clear that this refers **primarily** to the physical healing of our **physical bodies**.

> *That evening they brought to Him* **(Jesus)** *many who were oppressed by demons, and he cast out the spirits with a word and healed all who were sick. This was to fulfill what was spoken by the prophet Isaiah: "He took our illnesses and bore our diseases."* (Mat 8:15-17)

Just as the cross reveals true value God places upon our salvation, His suffering at the whipping post reveals how much it means to God to heal us from sickness, disease, and pain. Our healing is extremely costly and extremely valuable. If Jesus suffered stripes at the whipping post to pay for our physical healing, how could it even be possible for God to refuse the healing the Son purchased for us? *"He who did not spare his own Son but gave him up for us all, how will he not also with him graciously give us all things?"* (Rom. 8:32)

When Jesus rose from the dead He won victory over all the power of evil for us, because God redeemed us from the oppression of Satan. Jesus Christ is the perfect revelation of God and the will of God for everyone.

STAYING ON THE PATH

There have been times that I have not seen the finished work of Jesus manifest in people's lives. In one incident, there were three a young ladies I met in Cambodia who appeared to be around twenty years old. Each of them had been 100 percent deaf since birth.

When I laid hands on the first one, her immediately they opened and she began to scream. I was ministering through interpreters, so when I saw her excitement, I told the interpreters to ask her some questions without using any sign language. They told me, "She doesn't understand the Cambodian either, because she has never heard our language." This young lady continued to raise her voice in joy of hearing herself and others for the first time, while she signed to her friends, "I can hear! I can hear! I can speak! I can speak!"

Yet the next two girls did not receive their hearing that day though I ministered to them in the same way. One received partial improvement in one ear and the other experienced no improvement. As I traveled home with my ministry team that night, my host asked me, "Why did only one of the three get healed tonight?" This is the place where believers face a big temptation to begin to go off the path and begin to say things that aren't according to Jesus Christ.

What are our options? I suppose I could've blamed God and said something like, "It wasn't God's timing" but that isn't according to Christ. Did Jesus ever send anyone away saying, "I'm sorry. It's not God's time for you." When we don't see people receive their healing, don't slander the character of God just to save face.

Others make a different but equally damaging mistake. They don't blame God for people not getting healed. They do something just as bad. They blame the people who needed to be healed! I've encountered many people who have needed healing who have also said to me, "My pastor (or some other leader) told me that the reason that I've not been healed is because I don't have enough faith or have unconfessed sin in my life." Did Jesus ever do such a thing? Did He send people away unable to heal them because they had sin in their life or didn't have enough faith? My Bible says that Jesus sometimes healed people and said, "Go and sin no more" (Jn. 5:14) which is a strong indication that Jesus healed people that He knew were in sin. Think about it… entire villages and hillsides of people coming to Jesus for healing… all of them walking away healed. Do you think some of them might have had sin in their life or some doubts in their hearts? Yet Jesus healed them all.

I recently had the pleasure of meeting one of my long time heros in the faith, brother David Hogan. At the time of this conference, he reported that God had used him to raise 33 people from the dead. He also shared the story of the first time he saw the dead raised. In the process of sharing his story of the very first time he saw the dead raised, brother David said something very profound.

He said,

> "You need to understand that up till now, I had been preaching that Jesus Christ has authorized His disciples to heal the sick and raise the dead for years.(see Matt. 10:7-8) We were seeing people healed, but we kept burying our dead. My only proof that God wanted us to raise the dead was the Word of God. Outside of this, I had absolutely NO proof. None! But the difference between seeing the dead raised and you is staying on the path. I never believed that just because I wasn't seeing it happen yet meant that God didn't expect me to do it. I just needed to stay on the path of faith and obedience!"

Blaming God and blaming people who need our help is the wrong path. Let's let the devil take the blame for sickness and disease (like the Bible says… see Acts 10:38). Meanwhile, we must take the responsibility to stay on the path of obedience and faith. If we don't see people's condition change, *we will be the ones who are changing*… so long as we keep moving forward on the path of obedience and faith. By refusing to compromise the revelation of God that we have received in Jesus Christ, and continuing to take the responsibility and privilege we have to walk in the fullness of Jesus Christ, we will continue to grow up into the image of Jesus Christ in every respect.

Recently I was doing an exercise program and was struck by something that the exercise instructor said as he introduced the class. He said, "the only way to succeed in this class is to fail." He had my attention. How do you succeed by failing? I soon found out. We did lifts until we couldn't lift anymore. We did pushups until we collapsed on the floor. We did pull-ups until we dropped off the bar. We *succeeded* by failing.

I've discovered that working your muscles to the point of failure can be painful. That's part of the growth process— pushing through the pain. Yet, as I've continued with this exercise program, I find that I'm able to make it a lot further down the path before I hit that failure point.

It's very similar when it comes to growing up in the fullness of Jesus Christ. I'm not always sure why people don't receive healing. I *do know* that God isn't the hold up. Healing has already been purchased in full through Jesus Christ and made fully available in the presence of the Holy Spirit. Nor is it right to blame the people that need to be set free. Nor is it right to start blaming myself in such a way that I'm taking condemnation onto myself.

I've also found that analyzing myself or the situation doesn't help. What does help is that I continue keep exercising my faith, even if I'm exercising it "to the point of failure." I keep believing Jesus for everything His Word shows me that He has done, knowing that He's able to do it through me and in this situation. Sitting on the couch analyzing my fat belly doesn't help me get in shape. I need to get off the couch and exercise my body. Don't get pulled off the path of obedience and faith by trying to "figure out why you're not seeing the healing" for which you are believing God.

Don't let what you aren't seeing in your ministry change my mind about what God shows you in His Word that He has authorized you to do. Just forget what lies behind, and keep pressing forward on the path of obedience and faith, doing all that you can to grow up into the full measure of Jesus Christ! You have everything you need to heal the sick and manifest the victory of Jesus Christ in every situation.

When I first began exercising, I began very out of shape. The first day I began to work out, I was grunting, groaning, wobbling, gasping, and sweating all the way through the *warm up* exercising for the *real work out*. But as I continued to discipline myself to work out each day, I began to find that I was now able to do entire workouts with relative ease. Had I magically received muscles that I wasn't born with? Had I somehow received a "supernatural impartation of exercise anointing"? Of course not! I simply had begun to regularly use what I always had.

When God encourages us to "be strengthened in the grace that is in Christ Jesus" He illustrates this point by the analogy of soldiers remaining free from civilian pursuits, an athlete in competition and a hard-working farmer (see 2 Tim. 1-6). This shows us that the way to grow in spiritual power is similar to my experience in exercising my body. When you were born again, you received the power of the Holy Spirit and the victory of Jesus Christ. Now, discipline yourself to live only by His life, to agree only with His thoughts, to say only what He says, and to do only what He does through you. Stay on the path of grace, faith, and obedience in the confidence that even when you may not be seeing the healing take place, don't back down or slow down. Keep pressing forward for all that you see in Jesus until you see it in you!

Meanwhile, refrain from "junk food" words and attitudes— things like "Why isn't this changing?" "What's wrong with me?" "I'm so sick of this?" and, "What's taking so long?" Don't make the mistake of declaring your healing in the morning, then worrying the rest of the day. Align your whole heart and mind with Jesus Christ. He's bigger than anything you're facing… and He's inside of you! Discipline yourself to fix the eyes of your heart on Him, to filter your attitudes and thoughts by what you see in Him— not your situation.

There are people alive today because I didn't leave the path of obedience and faith after the first time I was unsuccessful at getting someone up off their deathbed. There are people who are leading healthy, pain free lives today that would still be in misery had I left the path of obedience and faith the first time I didn't see someone healed. Even though I was exercising my faith "to the point of failure", as I continue to stay on the path, I'm finding that I continue to get further and further down the path… and so will you if you continue to "walk just as He walked".

CHAPTER 4

DOES GOD CAUSE SICKNESS
OR HEAL IT?

Once I was at a Christian conference and a friend of mine pulled me aside because a family had arrived from a long distance away with a young girl who was unable to walk. She had been born with cerebral palsy. They wanted me to come and minister to her, so that she could be healed. My friends didn't come to get me because I had some 'special healing anointing.' They came to get me because they knew I have a heart for children and a gift to help them feel at ease as we are ministering to them.

When I got towards the back of the room, I was introduced to Anya. She was seven years old and was born with cerebral palsy. She was a very sweet little girl, but physically weak and unable to stand without leaning on something, and unable to walk more than a step or two without falling. She also suffered from regular seizures.

We began to lay hands on Anya and exercise the authority and power of the Kingdom of God for her healing. There were about three of us who took the lead in ministering to Anya. We worked as a team, with each of us taking turns for a few minutes, then stepping away and allowing the next one to continue to release the power of the Holy Spirit into Anya's body for healing. We also periodically stopped and told Anya, "Let's walk now, and see how you are doing." We kept this up for close to thirty minutes with little visible results.

I still remember the hotel manager watching us with a condescending smirk as the name of "Jesus" reverberated through the conference hotel lobby as we ministered to Anya. But his smirk changed to astonishment when this precious little girl began walking freely and even running around in the hotel lobby! Anya's healing made a huge surge forward that evening.

Everyone was so excited to see the joy on Anya's face as she walked and played games to continue exercise her new found strength and coordination! She left the hotel lobby with an over the shoulder mischievous glance at her parents saying, "Race you to the car!" That evening, after she got home, she ran around in the backyard with her brother and sisters— something she had never been able to do before! Anya has remained free from seizures for the past two years and has continued to walk strong forwards, backwards, and sideways, including up and down stairs. Praise the Lord!

Believe it or not, there are some people with "religious mindsets" that would be happy that the girl got healed but be upset with me. Why would they be upset with me, you might ask? Because I had skipped a session of this Christian conference to minister to this little girl. If you got in a discussion with one of these "religiously minded" people, they could probably convince you that I was in the wrong: "It's so rude, after someone has prepared a message from God, to be hanging out in the hallway disturbing other people. He could've prayed for her at another time."

Jesus is no friend of religion. Before Jesus came on the scene, humanity was walking in darkness, with only faint glimmers of light. Humanity's darkness was so thick, that when Jesus arrived to shine the true light, even those who were leaders among the people of God and teachers of the Word of God rejected and killed the very Son of God. When they crucified Jesus, they were convinced they were in the right and had Biblical support for their decision. They were certain they had Bible verses that proved that Jesus was wrong.

Here's a list of things that "Jesus did wrong":

- multiple accounts of healing people on the Sabbath
- claiming God was His own Father, making Himself to be the Son of God

- allowing His disciples to pick grain and eat on the Sabbath and without ceremonial hand washing
- showing mercy, even eating and drinking with sinners
- instead of "supporting God's appointed leaders", He exposed their hypocrisy for loving their power, prestige, and money more than God and people

Before the arrival of the Son of God to planet earth, if someone was born blind, deaf or lame, it was assumed to be "God's will" for them. Everyone thought, "If God made them this way, that must be the way God wants them to be." It was assumed that they would live the rest of their lives with these conditions. Those born blind would never see. The deaf would never here. The lame would never walk. And religious people attributed all this to "the will of God".

Unfortunately, here we stand two-thousand years after the advent of the Christ, and the religious world is still "comforting" those born with defects and their parents by telling them, "This is God's special plan for you," and "I know it's hard sometimes, but this is for God's glory," or, "You must be very special for God to give you such a heavy burden to carry." When people have their lives disrupted by a diagnosis of a deadly or chronic disease, Christians are often encouraged to accept this as "God's will" with the assurance, "God works everything for our good".

All this sounds very sweet, Biblical, and even loving… until Jesus shows up on the scene and **demonstrates the will of God.**

> **the blind receive their sight** and **the lame walk**, *lepers are cleansed and* **the deaf hear**, *and the dead are raised up, and the poor have good news preached to them. And* **blessed is the one who is not offended by me."** (Matt. 11:5-6)

Those walking in darkness often have strong notions of God, but haven't come to know the Father through Jesus Christ. As a result, they assume that God wants people who are suffering at the hands of sickness, disease, or defect to have that condition. They don't appreciate having their darkness exposed by someone showing up with the power and love of God to heal and set them free. Some, like the religious leaders of Jesus' day, would rather attribute miracles to demonic power than to admit that the power of God is working through someone that is not affiliated with their denomination. (Matt. 9:34) This is how Jesus got Himself crucified by Bible teachers. Why is this?

Because, in order to have faith for such a thing requires that you have come to know God, not merely as creator (which is common to all religions), but also as the Father who has revealed Himself in Jesus Christ. You are no longer merely expecting to meet God when you die, but you have come to realize that you have already died and been raised up with Christ. You are now living to manifest God through your life here and now. While the rest of the world accepts the oppression imposed by the works of darkness, you are rising up to set the prisoners free and destroy the works of the devil. You have begun to recognize the magnitude of Christ's victory and are zealous to enforce the enemy's defeat. You are manifesting the new creation in Christ (not just talking about it!) and have become a living rebuke to the powers of darkness! In other words, when you rise up to take a stand to enforce healing in the Name of Jesus, you've become a real threat to the domain of darkness.

Devils recognize when believers begin to contend for this ground in the Kingdom and are working desperately to maintain their deceptive strongholds. They've long enjoyed this quiet place to rest undisturbed, while they glut their destructive appetites to steal, kill, and destroy precious lives on earth, with no one to even whisper a single rebuke against them. Instead of engaging these devils in battle, we've been hoodwinked into a "peace treaty" by attributing these torturous conditions to God Himself as some sort of a "blessing in disguise."

BLIND FROM BIRTH

This demonic deception is nothing new. It's been around for a long time. Jesus dealt with it Himself when His disciples encountered a man who was born blind. Instead of doing something to help the man recover his sight through Kingdom resources, they started doing what most men do who don't understand the Kingdom of God— they started a theological discussion.

And his disciples asked him, "Rabbi, who sinned, this man or his parents, that he was born blind?" (John 9:2)

Do you see the assumptions embedded in this question? Let me spell out some of mindsets latent in their question, "Who made God mad? This guy, or his parents?" In other words, because this man was born blind, they assumed that God made him blind. Knowing that God is a just God, they assumed that God would not unjustly afflict anyone with blindness. So now, they are left to find out "Who sinned? Who made God angry? Was it the parents? Or this man?"[1] Very simply, they believed that the man's blindness was from God, so they were left to "theologize" about the reason that God made the man blind, while never examining their assumption that God was the cause of the man's blindness.

What was the result of this theological discussion? The man stayed blind. And so it goes today…

Thankfully, Jesus doesn't treat the misfortunes of others, even those who are *born with defect*, as an opportunity to have a theological debate. Watch what He does!

Jesus answered, "It was not that this man sinned, or his parents, but that the works of God might be displayed in him. We must work the works of him who sent me while it is day; night is coming, when no one can work. As long as I am in the world, I am the light

---

[1] This does NOT indicate that Jews or Jesus believed in reincarnation, where sins of a "past life" were causing afflictions in this life. It indicated that their view of God understood that God is not bound by time. Taking this into account, it was conceivable for God to see a "future sin" and punish the man in advance with blindness from birth on the basis of what he foresaw (speaking according to their deceived mindset that birth defect was punishment from God).

of the world." Having said these things, he spit on the ground and made mud with the saliva. Then he anointed the man's eyes with the mud and said to him, "Go, wash in the pool of Siloam" (which means Sent). So he went and washed and came back seeing. (John 9:2-7)

Jesus refused to engage in a theological discussion when there was someone in need who needed His help. He quickly put their question to rest and **demonstrated what everyone needed to know about God— He doesn't make people blind. He is our healer.**

This becomes even more clear once you punctuate the passage correctly. As it stands in most translations, it reads, *"Jesus answered, "It was not that this man sinned, or his parents, but that the works of God might be displayed in him. We must work the works of him who sent me while it is day; night is coming, when no one can work."* Breaking up the phrases with this sort of punctuation gives you the impression that the reason for the man's blindness is *"that the works of God might be displayed in him",* which would lead one to believe that God is allowing people to suffer affliction or to be born with defect for the sole reason that He wants to show His works in their life. But even if you believe that God allowed this (and I don't for reasons I will shortly share) there is *absolutely no way* anyone could use this passage with integrity to teach that God allows people to suffer from a lifelong condition that is never rectified by His grace and power. If you want to use this passage to justify God allowing sicknesses for His glory (which I do NOT), you must also conclude, based on Jesus' response, that **God's only way to glorify Himself in regards to these afflictions is** *to display His works by healing them through the power of Jesus Christ!*

However, I believe that there is a better way of understanding this passage. I believe the passage is best understood by adjusting the punctuation. Keep in mind, Bible translators are not "translating" Greek commas and periods into English punctuation marks. There is no punctuation in the Greek manuscripts. All punctuation is purely a matter of the interpretation of the translators, which is strongly influenced by their own doctrinal positions.

Watch what happens when we keep the words exactly as they are, and simply adjust the punctuation. *"Jesus answered, "It was not that this man sinned, or his parents.* **(Period. Jesus begins a new sentence to launch into a call to action)** *But that the works of God might be displayed in him,* **we** *must work the works of Him who sent me while it is day; night is coming, when no one can work."* When you read the passage with this punctuation, Jesus doesn't offer any explanation for the cause of the man's blindness. He simply points out the errors in the disciple's question, "Nobody sinned. Sin wasn't the cause of the blindness." Instead of offering an explanation for the man's blindness, Jesus launches into a call to action! "If you want to see the works of God displayed in this man, we must work the works of God while we have an opportunity!"

In other words, "You guys are standing around doing nothing to help this man is because you are assuming that blindness is a work of God. But if you want to see the work of God, you need to do something! God has appointed you to be His image bearers, the agents of His Kingdom on the earth. Take the opportunity to do the works of God while you have an opportunity! I am the Light of the World, a container to shine forth My Father's works. Watch and learn the Father's works." Then Jesus heals the man. Boom!

Jesus' answer was action! He didn't waste time engaging the disciples in theological discussion. Instead He *became the answer* to their question! He provided the solution for the man's blindness! How much of our "church chatter" is simply irrelevant to the real mission of the Kingdom of God? Our analyzing the problem doesn't help solve it. Analyzing God isn't the same thing as believing and obeying Him.

Jesus is calling His disciples, which includes you and me, to stop blaming God or blaming people for physical afflictions. The church must stop wasting precious time in endless theological chatter and analytical inactivity that never moves out in the power of the Kingdom of God to help people. Sitting around analyzing the situation isn't going to release the resources of the Kingdom of Heaven. We must fix our eyes upon Jesus Christ until we are filled with the light that is in Him. For now, *we* are "the light of the World." (Matt. 5:12) He is calling us to take our place as freedom fighters, to become vessels of God through whom He can display His image and accomplish His works of healing for those suffering under the oppression of the devil.

When Jesus Christ called Himself "the light of the world" He gave sight to a man born blind. He healed the man's condition and in doing so, the light of who God Himself is pierced the darkness. When Jesus calls His disciples, "the light of the World" Jesus is giving us His own identity as agents called to demonstrate the Kingdom of God, which includes healing all manner of sicknesses, including birth defects! God wants us not only to see the light of His glory but also to receive it, be filled with it, and pour it out. God wants to put Himself on display through our lives just as He did through Jesus. For this to happen, we must embrace God's identity for us as His image bearers on the earth and become agents of His healing power.

Through the gospel, we have access to resources far greater than the medical system. We will never accept the limits of human understanding as the limits of our own faith regarding what God is able to heal. Isn't our God "*able to do far more abundantly than all that we ask or think, according to the power at work within us*?" (Eph. 3:19-20)

We are not of those who lean on our own understanding! We are those who "acknowledge Him in all our ways", and as we acknowledge Him in all our ways, we teach body parts, D.N.A., and demons to acknowledge Him also. Jesus Christ is King! God is our Healer and nothing is impossible for Him! Jesus Christ bore all sickness, defect, disease and affliction in His body at the whipping post. He carried ALL sickness so that we can be healed.

JESUS IS BIGGER THAN HIS OWN BIBLE

Is there any reason to believe that God excludes anyone, even those born with conditions?

In my ministry, I have had several people bring up God's Words to Moses, when the LORD said to him, "*Who has made man's mouth? Who makes the mute, or deaf, or seeing, or blind? Is it not I, the LORD?*" (Exo. 4:10-11, KJV)

The first time someone brought this up to me, I was actually ministering healing for a condition they had suffered since birth. (That's a strange way to encourage someone who is seeking to exercise faith for your healing! I don't advise you follow this example. I'm sometimes amazed how quick Christians are to pull out Bible verses that seem to support staying sick! It's almost like they are fighting to stay sick, miserable, and in pain. Is it any wonder they experience so little of God's power when the Word of God clearly shows that God's power operates *through faith*?) At that time, I had no answer readily available.

Since then, I've looked closely at this verse and discovered a couple of important truths. First, if you read this verse closely, God is not claiming to make the defects. He's proclaiming that He makes all people, including those afflicted with birth defects. God is not claiming to be the cause of the defect. He is claiming to be the creator of all people, including those born with birth defects or limitations. God is not saying, "I afflict people with birth defects, so you can trust me." That makes no sense! God is telling Moses, "I made everyone. I know everyone's limitations. I know my options. I chose you to be my deliverer for Israel."

I was born a sinner, yet God made me. Does that mean that I was born the way God wants me? Jesus shows us that, no matter how we are born, we need to be born again by the power of God's Spirit. If we need healing, the same suffering that purchased our forgiveness and the gift of the Holy Spirit, also purchased our physical healing.

But more importantly, we must remember that this verse was in Jesus' Bible too! While at first, this may seem insignificant, it's anything but! Jesus jumps right over this verse affirming God as our Creator to fully manifest the Father in a much larger way. Jesus is a bigger revelation of God than even His own Bible.

As we hold this verse up to full light of the Father we see in Jesus Christ, do we see the Father in the Son making people blind? Do we see Him making people deaf? On the contrary, we see *"great crowds came to him, bringing with them the lame, the blind, the crippled, the mute, and many others, and they put them at his feet, and* **he healed them, so that the crowd wondered, when they saw the mute speaking, the crippled healthy, the lame walking, and the blind seeing. And they glorified the God of Israel**." (Mat 15:30-31)

When great crowds came forward filled with people with serious conditions, did Jesus sort through them, "Anyone who was born with a condition, please step aside so that I can heal those who were not afflicted since birth?" Do we ever see Jesus turning anyone away for healing quoting, "Have you never read what God said to Moses at the burning bush? Do we see the Son rebuking people for seeking His healing touch for birth defects? Why would you reject God's purpose and plan for you in exercising His prerogative to make you blind, or deaf or mute?" Do we ever see Jesus doing any such thing? Or do we ever see Jesus laying hands on pregnant women to offer a "blessing" saying, "May this child be blessed to be blind, deaf or lame?" No? Then why do we say such things about our Father in heaven?

The passage about the burning bush was in Jesus' Bible too. But Jesus is bigger than His Bible. All that had been revealed up to that time pointed to Jesus, but they were mere shadows. He is the substance.

What Jesus Christ accomplished through His suffering is available for everyone! He has purchased forgiveness and the gift of the Holy Spirit for sinners. He has purchased healing for those who are sick, including those born with birth defect. He ministered healing freely to all who had need of healing. He never excluded anyone with any sickness, any disease, or defect.

Yet many of us have been taught that the ministry of healing was only for special people— like Jesus and the apostles— or for a limited period of time— like before the completion of the Bible. Others have believed in healing, but have never seen God's power working through them to heal the sick consistently. You need some practical training and coaching. We will begin to focus on these issues in the following chapters, so that God can do the same thing through you… and even more!

CHAPTER 5

WHO WILL GOD USE TO HEAL TODAY?

You may not realize it yet, but if you are a believer in Jesus Christ, no matter how desperate your situation may be, you already have all the help and power you need living inside of you—*"Christ in you, the hope of glory."* (Col. 1:27) Be encouraged! You have the greatest miracle worker that the world has ever seen living inside of you, and He is still healing the sick today, just as He has always done.

A couple of years ago, this lesson was demonstrated powerfully to me on a visit to a village in Cambodia. I had just spent the morning walking through the village small team healing the sick and proclaiming the good news of Jesus Christ along with a small team. This team included one young man, who, along with his wife, were the only Christian family in the entire village.

As we went back to his hut for lunch, he mentioned that he needed healing for pain in his knee. So I called his wife over and told her that I want her to learn how to heal by practicing on her husband. She objected saying, "I haven't been walking with you this morning, so I haven't heard your teaching. I don't think this will work." I replied to her, "That is no problem. I can show you easily. It's not complicated." I asked her, "Are you born again?" She answered affirmatively. "So does Jesus Christ live inside of you?" She said "Yes." Then I said, "Do you believe that Jesus Christ is able to heal your husband, and that He wants your husband's knee healed?" She said, "Yes." So I said, "Then He'll do this through you!"

Then I coached her through the process. I said, "I want you to put your hand on your husband's knee, but as you do this, I want you to believe that your hand is the hand of Jesus Christ. You are His body. Correct?" So she placed her hand on her husband's knee.

Now I said, "Instead of praying and asking God to heal your husband, we are going to believe that you get to speak to your husband's knee in the Name of Jesus Christ. When you speak, heaven's power is being released to bring your words to pass." So I had her repeat after me. "Say this," I said, "In the Name of Jesus, all pain go. Knee be healed!"

Then I told her husband to move his knee. He reported that he noticed no change. At this point, his wife looked at me ready to give up and said, "See, I must not be doing it right." But I looked at her and said, "God is working. Just do it again." She did… with the same results— no change! I encouraged her to do it once more, and she did. When her husband moved his knee, this time, he reported, "Now that's better. Still a little pain left, but much better!" Now, without me prompting, his wife continued, "Right now! In the Name of Jesus, I tell you pain, Come out! Knee, be completely healed!" When her husband moved his knee, there was no pain. He walked on it the rest of the day with no pain, and when we returned the next day, his knee continued to function perfectly pain free for the first time in several years since he injured his knee in a motorcycle accident.

Here's the point… her husband's knee was healed, NOT through me, but through his own wife who discovered the reality that Jesus Christ was able to heal through her. Experience has shown me this same thing repeatedly— people are living with pain and sickness needlessly because they never knew who they were in Christ and how to walk in His power.

How many people are waiting on *you* to discover who you are in Christ so that you can set them free in Jesus' Name?

Jesus Christ never sent anyone out to proclaim the gospel with mere words. He always sent them out with the authority to demonstrate the Kingdom's power to set captives free. Even after Jesus had gone to the cross and arose victoriously over the grave, Jesus would not allow His well-trained disciples to go and preach the gospel. He "ordered them not to depart from Jerusalem, but to wait for the promise of the Father," the Holy Spirit who would give them "power to be His witnesses" (Acts. 1:5,8).

To be a witness of Jesus Christ, we *must* demonstrate His power. We need the Holy Spirit. We must be completely yielded, saturated, and clothed with another person. Without demonstrating the power of Jesus Christ in the power of the Holy Spirit, no matter how or what we are preaching, we are *not* the witness of Jesus Christ that He had in mind. He envisioned people carrying His own presence and power as they proclaimed His glory. Jesus envisioned people setting captives free from the grip of sickness and sin as they proclaimed His victory over evil.

Some Christians come from backgrounds where they were taught that God no longer intends to work in His miraculous power through believers today, because now we have the Bible. They suppose that miracles were needed only to validate the Bible, and once the Bible's authority is established miracles are no longer needed. Because they hold to this view, anyone who claims that God is working through them to heal the sick is treated with a great deal of suspicion and sometimes outright hostility, since in their view, this would give them authority to speak for God like the original New Testament writers. There's one BIG problem with this though… this view is never taught in the Bible… **anywhere**! In fact, the Bible specifically teaches otherwise.

Everyone knows the Bible verse John 3:16 which says, *"For God so loved the world, that he gave his only Son, that whoever believes in him should not perish but have eternal life."* But a few chapters later in the same book Jesus says, "*Truly, truly, I say to you, **whoever** believes in me will also do the works that I do; and greater works than these will he do, because I am going to the Father.*" (John 14:12) Did you see that? The same people that receive eternal life (i.e. "whoever believes") are the same people who get to do the miraculous works of Jesus Christ and even greater. So we could condense these verses to read,

> **"*For God so loved the world, that He gave His only Son, that whoever believes in Him should not perish but have eternal life and do the works that Jesus does, and even greater works because Jesus has gone to the Father!*"**

After Jesus rose from the dead, He commissioned His disciples to go out.

Mark 16:15-18 And he said to them, "*Go into all the world and proclaim the gospel to the whole creation. **Whoever believes** and is baptized will be saved… and* *these signs will accompany **those who believe**: in my name they will cast out demons; they will speak in new tongues; they will pick up serpents with their hands; and if they drink any deadly poison, it will not hurt them; they will lay their hands on the sick, and they will recover."*

> *God so loved the world that He gave His only Son that whoever believes in Him would have eternal life and do the works that He did, and even greater.*

When you hear someone speaking on the phone, often you can get a good idea of what the person on the other end of the line is saying simply by listening to one side of the conversation. Judging by the signs that Jesus said would accompany those who believe the apostle's message, what can we tell about the content of the message that the apostles proclaimed?

Jesus obviously expected that the gospel that He was sending the apostles out to proclaim would produce people who cast out demons, spoke in tongues, exercised divine dominion, experienced supernatural protection, and healed the sick. According to Jesus, these are for everyone who believed the apostles message and was baptized in water.

MIRACLES POINT TO JESUS, NOT OURSELVES

We know from the rest of the New Testament that genuine believers could also be deceived and make serious mistakes. So then, supernatural signs are **not** an indication of flawless doctrine, a holy life, or spiritual authority in the church. God's power operates by grace through faith in the finished work of Jesus Christ as an indication that you are real a believer in the original message of the apostles- and not a special sort of believer, just a "whoever believes" sort of believer.

In fact, there are indications that it's possible to exercise faith for miracles without genuine faith for salvation. As an example, take Judas Iscariot. Do you think he healed the sick and cast out demons with the rest of the disciples? Had he been the only one that never had any miracles take place, it probably would have been a "no brainer" at the last supper for the disciples to figure out the identity of the son of perdition who was betraying Jesus. But this simply wasn't the case. There will be many like Judas on the last day who say 'Lord, Lord, did we not prophesy in your name, and cast out demons in your name, and do many mighty works in your name?' And Jesus will declare to them, 'I never knew you; depart from me, you workers of lawlessness.' (Matt. 7:21-23)

So never allow your own heart to turn a blind eye towards sin in your life simply because God is still using you to work miracles. Endeavor always to walk in holiness "without which no one will see the Lord." (Heb. 12:14) Nor should you allow yourself to be manipulated or deceived by someone simply because God uses them for genuine miracles "as though by our own power or piety." (Acts 3:12) God will use some pretty messed up believers simply because Jesus is Lord and God loves people. Just look at the churches of Galatia and Corinth, both of which had fallen into serious error, yet miracles were continuing to take place in their midst (1 Cor. 12:10, Gal. 3:5). So let's walk in holiness, test everything by the Word of God, and never allow the enemy to intimidate us through his accusations that God won't use us because of sin in our lives. If He will use Judas, the legalistic Galatians, and the fleshly Corinthians to demonstrate His power, He will use you!

WHO DO YOU SEE IN THE MIRROR?

The biggest obstacle that Christians face in divine healing is not demons, diseases, or unconfessed sins. It is mindsets that stem from a failure to grasp the significance of our union with Christ.

We call ourselves "sinners saved by grace" when the word of God calls us "saints." Much of the prayer life of the church has been reduced to begging God to do what He's already done or asking God to do something He's told us to do. Many believers spend countless hours crying out to God for Him to "pour out His Spirit" and "send revival" or "send your healing power" all because we've failed to understand and believe what God has already given us in Christ. There is no place that a sense of spiritual inferiority comes to the surface more quickly than when believers are encouraged to believe that God will use them to heal the sick just like Jesus.

The Christian life is lived by renewing our mind to the mind of Christ, so that we adopt His mindset in every area of life. Our mindsets will change once we grasp the true nature of the Christian life. Our Christian life is not primarily our character, our beliefs, our lifestyle or even our service to God. Our Christian life is the supernatural life of Jesus Christ that God put inside us when we were born again. This is our Christian life. It's the same supernatural life that raised Jesus Christ from the dead. It's an unshakable, permanent life. This is the life that pulsated within His innermost being every day of His life and flowed out in wisdom, love, and truth. The very life that was implanted by the Holy Spirit inside the virgin womb of Mary has been implanted by the Holy Spirit inside of us as our life. In other words, our Christian life is not just a new lifestyle to adopt. It's a new life form to contain and partake in— the divine life of God.

He has granted to us his precious and very great promises, so that through them you may become **partakers of the divine nature***, having escaped from the corruption that is in the world because of sinful desire.* (2Pe 1:4)

But he who is joined to the Lord becomes **one spirit with him***.*
(1Co 6:17)

When **Christ who IS your life** *appears, then you also will appear with him in glory.* (Col 3:4)

I have been crucified with Christ. **It is no longer I who live, but Christ who lives in me***. And the life I now live in the flesh* **I live by the faith of the Son of God** *(lit. greek), who loved me and gave himself for me.* (Gal 2:20)

If **we live by the Spirit***, let us also keep in step with the Spirit.*
(Gal 5:25)

God created you to be the host of another life form. You were created to contain and express divinity, God's very own presence on the earth. God created you to express His likeness and gave you authority to accomplish His will.

*Then God said, "Let us make man **in our image, after our likeness. And let them have dominion… over all the earth** and over every creeping thing that creeps on the earth."* (Gen 1:26)

This is how Jesus Christ lived. He lived as a container of the life of His Father, exercising the dominion of man in union with (instead of rebellion against) the Kingdom of God. Through Jesus Christ, you have been recovered to fulfill this very purpose! Jesus Christ did not come to improve your old life. He came to set you free from your old life and put a brand new life inside of you with a brand new identity.

In order to do this, He had to set you free from yourself. He did this by becoming one with your old self, so that when He was crucified, you were crucified in Him. (Gal. 2:20) He became one with you in flesh and blood so that you could become one Spirit with Him! He didn't come merely to give you more information about God that you can use to overcome evil, or to give you a set a principles that can be reduced into a formula for healing the sick and working miracles. Jesus Christ came to overcome evil by the power of His Spirit and then put His victorious life inside of you so that you can walk in the power of His reigning life. (Rom. 5:17)

THE CART OF HEALING AND THE HORSE OF YOUR IDENTITY IN CHRIST

We don't get our identity from what we see happening (or not happening) in our ministry. Our identity in Christ is based completely upon our spiritual union with Him through faith. Our confidence in our union with Jesus Christ is 'the horse' that supplies the power to 'pull the cart' of healing!

When Jesus disciples returned after He sent them out two by two to heal the sick and proclaim the Kingdom in the villages of Israel, they returned with joy, saying, *"Lord, even the demons are subject to us in your name!"* (Luke 10:17). After Jesus affirmed their authority over demons, Jesus warned them about misplacing their identity in ministry results. He said, *"Nevertheless, do not rejoice in this, that the spirits are subject to you, but rejoice that your names are written in heaven."* (Luke 10:20). Our identity is fixed in heaven and is the only sure footing for our joy.

One evening my son and I were at a church praying for people who needed healing. As we wrapped up and got in the car I asked him, "How are you doing buddy? How did it go for you tonight?" He sighed and said, "Honestly Dad, I'm trying not to be discouraged right now." I asked, "Why?" He replied, "I know that I have the same Holy Spirit as you do. I know that I'm as much of a child of God as you are. But I'm also noticing that you get more results than me when it comes to praying for healing."

I spoke up at this point, "Son, I don't get ANY results. None! And I suspect that if there is part of you that's discouraged about *not* getting results, then that's probably the same part of you that would have gotten puffed up and proud if you were seeing miracles happen tonight. So how about we do this— let's let Jesus Christ be the only one who gets any ministry results! Okay?" He smiled, "Okay Dad."

The next evening, my son and I were ministering in a church and a man who had suffered a blown out ear drum several years ago in an industrial accident came to my son for ministry. It was medically impossible for him to ever hear again. But my son laid hands on him and in the matter of just a couple of minutes the man's ear was completely healed! When we get ourselves out of the way, Jesus can flow through us to accomplish Jesus' results!

Although God got us out of the way 2,000 years ago when we were crucified with Christ, we must allow the power of that fact to operate in our daily lives. We simply fix our eyes on Jesus Christ and allow Him to be awesome in us and through us. If for some reason we're not seeing the healing Jesus paid for, that's no reason for us to start evaluating ourselves. Why start questioning ourselves based on the work of the enemy, when God wants us to know ourselves according to the work of Jesus Christ? We should just continue to "forget what lies behind and reach forward for what lies ahead," renewing our mind to the mind of Christ as we love God, love people with God's love, and crush the works of satan with all the resources of heaven!

You are authorized by heaven to heal the sick wherever there is a need, whatever the need may be. God is with you! Jesus Christ gives His disciples *"authority over unclean spirits, to cast them out, and to heal every disease and every affliction."* (Matt. 10:1) You have been given *"authority to tread on serpents and scorpions, and over all the power of the enemy, and nothing shall hurt you."* (Luke 10:19) *As He is so also are we in this world.* (1 Jn. 4:17) You are an ambassador of Jesus Christ with the authority to speak and act in His Name in every situation.

Last week, a friend of mine shared a personal story from his own experience that helped him understand his new identity in Christ. He told me, "I grew up with a deadbeat, absentee father. As I got older, I went to live with my dad one summer. I really wanted a bike, but didn't have the money. But my dad had this really old bike in the garage. So I started to fix it up. I replaced the handle bars, took off the rims, put on a new seat, gave it a paint job, but when I took it out for a test ride, the tire popped and I had to walk the bike back to the house. As it turned out, I had to go away for the weekend, so I asked my dad if he would mind replacing the tire for me so I could ride it when I got back. He said that he would be happy to help."

My friend continued, "As soon as I returned from my weekend away, the first thing I saw when I pulled into the driveway was the bike sitting in the garage right where I left it— with the same flat tire! My dad had done nothing! Immediately, my heart was flooded with all the years of frustration. I was so angry that I was cursing my father under my breath, feeling somewhere between rage and despair. I just needed to be alone so I ran up to my room. But as soon as I opened the door, I saw this amazing brand new bike. It was a top of the line BMX race bike, far better than anything I could've imagined ever owning. It was the first time in my life that I actually cried tears of joy— partially from the bike, but mostly because for the first time in my life I realized that my Dad actually loved me!"

Many Christians get very frustrated because they are trying to use God and the gospel to patch up their life and repair themselves. They become mighty discouraged when it seems like God isn't helping them. But the truth is that

God has purchased for us all a brand new life. It's a higher form of life—eternal life in fellowship with Him!

Our heavenly Father is waiting for us to leave the old bike in the garage and discover our new identity and power in Christ. God has given us a brand new relationship, a new Spirit, and a new identity. God has a top of the line life! He's given us the very relationship that He has with Jesus Christ *as our relationship with Him*. We've been adopted as sons of God through Jesus Christ. It's a gift for us to enjoy forever! He's also given us the very Spirit of Jesus Christ inside us as a brand new nature. No longer are we sinners. We are truly righteous in the core of our being. This is the basis of our true identity!

> *God sent forth his Son… to redeem those who were under the law, so that* **we might receive adoption as sons**. *And because* **you are sons**, *God has sent* **the Spirit of his Son into our hearts**, *crying, "Abba! Father!"* *So* **you are no longer a slave, but a son, and if a son, then an heir through God.** (Gal 4:4-7)

There is only one thing that I would adjust in this story to make it a more fitting illustration. We need to change the brand new BMX bike to a top of the line Harley Davidson! Not only do we have a 'new bike' to ride, this bike comes with power! You don't peddle a Harley Davidson down the street. Nor will you get anywhere by just studying and believing in your new Harley. Eventually you must sit yourself upon it, crank it up, point it the right direction, and open up the throttle. This can be a challenge, but not merely as challenging as trying to make an old bike with a flat tire ride like a Harley— which is exactly what most Christians are trying to do, because they've never grasped the wonderful mystery of our union with Jesus Christ.

So let's leave the 'old bike'— everything we were apart from Christ—in the garage. No need to repair it. No need to ever ride it again. It's old. We have a new identity, a new nature. We are new creations. Christ lives in us.

Christ is our identity! He is our new life! We are containers of Jesus Christ, living in His authority, power, and love.

CHAPTER 6

HOW DOES GOD HEAL TODAY?

JUST LIKE JESUS

It may surprise you to hear that Jesus Christ was not healing the sick because He had some special power or authority. Although He was fully divine, Jesus proclaimed repeatedly that every miracle was not by His own power or authority, but rather was a work of His Father. As the fully divine Son of God, He had set aside the use of any of His divine power or privilege to live among us as a man— man as God intended— a man who contained God.

In fact, many times He very explicitly stated that He was NOT able do miracles! Don't believe me?

> *So Jesus said to them, "Truly, truly, I say to you,* **the Son can do nothing of his own accord**... *(Joh 5:19)*

> ...**the Father** *who dwells in me* **does his works**. *(Joh 14:9-10)*

> ... **I do nothing on my own authority**, *but speak just as the Father taught me. And he who sent me is with me. He has not left me alone, for I always do the things that are pleasing to him." (Joh 8:27-29)*

It may surprise you to realize, that although Jesus is fully divine, His divinity gave Him **no** advantage when it came to healing the sick. Jesus lived among us purely as a human being with no more access to spiritual authority and power than He has given us now that we are born again. Jesus could only heal by the authority of someone else and the power of someone else, namely His Father, just like us.

Think of it like this. If the King of a nation decides to live for a period as a homeless man in order to understand and address the problem of homelessness and poverty in his nation, while the King is living on the streets as a homeless man, he would still be both King and a homeless man, would he not? But, while it is possible for the King to *be* the King and a homeless man at the same time, it's *not* possible for the King to *live as* a King and homeless man at the same time. The King must give up the castle, and the guards, and the fancy clothes, and the servants, and the advisors to live on the streets with only the clothes on his back and the wits in his head. Although He is fully divine, Jesus Christ completely set aside the exercise of His own divine power to live among us as a man, just like you and I. (Phil. 2:6-7)

Jesus arrived on planet earth as the "only begotten Son" of God. But He is the "only begotten" no longer! Now Jesus Christ is "the firstborn among many brothers." (Rom. 8:29) God has adopted you as a son, which means He's given you the same standing as if you were Jesus Christ Himself. If you are a believer in Jesus Christ, God has given you the same standing, same relationship, and same Spirit as the Lord Jesus Christ. This is the foundation of why God can heal the sick through you and any other believer in Christ!

God has made you brand new in His sight and put the Spirit of Jesus Christ inside of you. (Gal. 4:4-7) Every born again believer is the proud owner of a 'brand new Harley Davidson'— the personal presence of "Christ IN YOU" (Col. 1:27). God will do through you what He did through Jesus Christ... and even greater.

> *Therefore, as* **you received Christ Jesus the Lord, so walk in Him**... *See to it that no one takes you captive by philosophy and empty deceit, according to human tradition, according to the elemental spirits of the world, and not according to Christ.* (Col. 2:6-8)

God doesn't just want you only to receive Jesus Christ. He wants you to walk in Him. Don't just receive the Harley Davidson! Get on and ride! Take your seat in heavenly places in Christ, far above all powers and principalities, in absolute victory over all evil, completely accepted in the glorious love of the Father! (Eph. 2:6)

We are quite comfortable with Jesus being amazing in the Bible, but we must expect Jesus Christ to be no less amazing as He lives through us. Many people will try to give you logical reasons why you can't walk like Jesus Christ, but it's just empty deceit. You'll have to break with the traditions of your denomination, your family, and your culture to walk in the fullness of Jesus Christ, but it's worth it!

Remember speaking to your hand? It's time to declare God's truth about the rest of you! Say this, "I have received Jesus Christ the Lord. I walk in His power. I walk in His dominion and victory. I walk in His love. Christ lives in me. He lives through me. All that I am apart from Him was crucified 2,000 years ago. I am a container of the living God. I renew my mind to the mind of Christ. The Spirit of Jesus Christ cries out "Abba Father" in my heart. I am free from sin. I am spotless, blameless, and above reproach. I am the righteousness of God. Christ is my life. I contain the very image and likeness of God. The Father has given me the very same relationship with Him that Jesus has. I stand in the grace and favor of Jesus Christ. I walk in the fellowship of Jesus Christ. I walk in His power over sickness and disease. I exercise His authority over devils. Everything Jesus Christ can do, He can do through me. I walk as He walked. As He is, so am I in this world. He is amazing. He is amazing in me and through me today! He is love. I am love. He is unstoppable. I am unstoppable."

When the Goliaths of sickness, disease, and birth defects taunt you, trying to make you feel small saying, "Am I a dog that you come at me with sticks" you can charge ahead and say, "This day I will cut your head off, because I do not come against you in merely human resources, but in the mighty Name of Jesus Christ and the power of the Holy Spirit!" When you know who God says you are, nothing intimidates you.

WHO SPEAKS WHEN YOU TALK?

The most common mistake that Christians who believe in healing make when it comes to healing the sick is that they ask God to heal the sick. Instead of talking to God about the disease, we should be speaking to the disease on behalf of God. Jesus never prayed to God to ask Him to heal the sick. He manifested God to the sickness. Christ in you does the same thing. He expects you to do the same thing. As you align yourself with the same mindset as Jesus Christ, His Kingdom power and love will flow through you. This is a revolutionary insight for most Christians that will make a huge difference in the ministry of healing.

Although Jesus clearly said that He could not heal the sick by His own power or authority, and that healing was the work of the Father in Him, do we ever see Jesus laying His hand on someone saying, "Father, please come and touch them with your power right now?" No!

What do we see?
*And he stood over her and **rebuked the fever**, and it left her…* (Luke 4:39)

*And Jesus stretched out his hand and touched him, saying, **"I will; be clean."** And immediately his leprosy was cleansed.* (Matt. 8:3)

*Taking her by the hand he said to her, "Talitha cumi," which means, **"Little girl, I say to you, arise."*** (Mar 5:41)

In every instance in which we are given any detail on how Jesus healed the sick, we always see Him exercising authority over sickness, disease, and devils. When He spoke, He spoke in the Father's authority. Jesus tells us, *"For whatever the Father does, that **the Son does likewise**."* (John 5:19)

Jesus openly taught that He could not heal by His own authority or power. It was His Father healing through Him. Yet Jesus *never prayed* for anyone to be healed. He never asked God to do it! Instead Jesus acted and spoke in His Father's authority. He spoke and acted in union with His Father, and His Father acted in union with the Son. Jesus commanded His disciples to do the same thing, to speak and act in His authority and power. So instead of asking God to heal, we should follow the example of Jesus and the apostles to act and speak in His authority, commanding the sickness to depart, laying hands and believing for healing.

Instead of laying hands and saying, "God, please touch them and heal them," we should exercise Kingdom authority and say something like, "Sickness, go now! Be healed and whole in the Name of Jesus." We should be exercising Kingdom authority in faith. As T.L. Osborn said many times, "Never ask God to do something He's already done. And never ask God to do something He's told you to do." God healed the sick over 2,000 years ago when Jesus Christ suffered stripes on His back. God has commanded us to heal the sick. So let's walk in the blessing of what Jesus has already accomplished and obey what He's told us to do by following the example He gave us.

Jesus doesn't just depend upon the Father's power and authority. The Son must embody and manifest the Father's power and authority by doing exactly what He sees the Father doing. The Son is to bear the image of the Father and display the Father's likeness. Apparently Jesus never saw the Father begging someone else to help Him make sickness leave. On the contrary, the Son saw the Father exercising authority over sickness and disease to heal the sick. The Son did what He saw the Father do and exercised authority and released the Father's power to heal the sick.

But this is just for Jesus, right? What do the Scriptures say?

> *But Peter said, "I have no silver and gold, but what I do have I give to you.* **In the name of Jesus Christ of Nazareth, rise up and walk!"** (Acts 3:6)

> *And Peter said to him, "Aeneas,* **Jesus Christ heals you; rise and make your bed."** *And immediately he rose.* (Acts 9:34)

> *And this she kept doing for many days. Paul, having become greatly annoyed, turned and said to the spirit,* **"I command you in the name of Jesus Christ to come out of her."** *And it came out that very hour.* (Act 16:18)

Ananias, a devout man according to the law, well-spoken of by all the Jews who lived there, came to me, and standing by me said to me, **'Brother Saul, receive your sight.'** *And at that very hour I received my sight and saw him.* (Acts 22:12-13)

By faith in Christ, we have become sons and daughters of God. We must walk as Jesus Christ, our elder brother, walked. Follow the example of Jesus Christ and His disciples by addressing situations that aren't in line with God's will with Kingdom authority and commanding sickness and disease to depart.

Several times, Jesus taught His disciples specifically about the importance of addressing situations with Kingdom authority and faith in God. He spoke about this on several occasions and in one instance Jesus specifically applied these principles to the ministry of healing (Mat. 17:20). Let's take a look at what Jesus teaches us about releasing the power of God through our words.

And Peter remembered and said to him, "Rabbi, look! The fig tree that you cursed has withered." And Jesus answered them, **"Have faith in God.** *Truly, I say to you,* **whoever says to this mountain**, *'Be taken up and thrown into the sea,' and does not doubt in his heart, but* **believes that what he says will come to pass, it will be done for him**. *Therefore I tell you,* **whatever** *you ask in prayer, believe that you have received it, and it will be yours. And whenever you stand praying, forgive, if you have anything against anyone, so that your Father also who is in heaven may forgive you your trespasses."* (Mark 11:21-25)

Jesus was always addressing situations with words of authority, like commanding sickness, demons, and fig trees! Yet, when His disciples marveled at His authority, Jesus didn't say, "Hey guys, just forget about it. This is something special only for Me. I'm the Messiah, not you. You guys just need to work on your character and leave the supernatural stuff to Me." No! Jesus never said anything like this. On the contrary, Jesus told us that speaking with Kingdom authority is something for **whoever** has faith in

God and a mountain that needs to move! Do you have a mountain to move? Then this is good news indeed… if you are ready to have faith in God!

God works through us as we step into our created purpose to image forth God by speaking forth His will. You speak and God's Spirit is released to bring your words to pass. The presence of the Spirit may be "hovering on the waters" as in creation, but only as the word is spoken does He spring into action. Just as the Spirit executed the Father's word "Let there be light," the Father and the Son have now sent us the Holy Spirit to be our Helper! As Curry Blake says, "When a son of God speaks, heaven hears and agrees and hell hears and obeys." Our words point and shoot, but the Holy Spirit is the "bullet" that hits the target and destroys the works of the devil!

Towards God *we speak in gratitude.* We no longer ask God to give us anything out of a sense of lack, because He's already given us every spiritual blessing heaven has to offer in Christ. But we do ask God to enable us to see and walk in what we have received so that we may grow into the image of Christ and walk in His fullness. We have received Jesus Christ and the presence of the Kingdom of God. We've already received healing, salvation, and victory over all evil. We believe we have already received that for which we've asked, so we thank Him for it. One of the ways to express your confidence that you've received from God is to thank Him! "Thank you Jesus for perfect wholeness and healing!" or "Thank you Jesus that you've crushed down syndrome. Thank you for perfect D.N.A.."

Towards the situation *we speak with authority.* We command all things to bow before the Lord Jesus Christ to the glory of God the Father. We proclaim liberty to the captives and freedom for all who are oppressed by satan. We say, "Kingdom of God come!" We say, "Let the will of God be done on earth just as it is in heaven!" There are no blind eyes, deaf ears, mute tongues or lame legs in heaven. There is no cancer nor down syndrome. There are no heart murmurs, nor autism. These things didn't come from heaven. These are mountains that must be moved. God's plan to move them is YOU! God will move when you have faith in God and speak with confidence in Him.

Towards people *we embody God's redemptive love.* In order for God's power to flow through us freely, we must keep ourselves out of the way. If we are judging people, holding on to hurt feelings, and criticizing people, we will find ourselves standing on the hose wondering why there is only a trickle of water coming out. God's Kingdom power operates by grace. Let your heart be filled with heaven's mercy and grace and you'll find His Kingdom working through you.

When my friends and I ministered to little Anya, we never asked God to heal her. We didn't do a "spiritual background check" to see if her dad was a Mason, or whether her parents were "in faith." We ministered to her in the confidence that Jesus Christ healed her 2,000 years ago at the whipping post. We didn't need to petition heaven to get God to give us anything. We already had everything inside of us that Anya needed to be healed. It was our job to release healing to Anya as ambassadors of Jesus Christ.

As we laid hands on Anya, we spoke with authority to the powers of darkness affecting her body and to her body itself. We said things like, "In the Name of Jesus, I release life into Anya's body. Be strong, be whole. I command coordination through the body. All oppression and infirmity, you go! Now! Thank you Jesus for complete wholeness for Anya. Now, be whole in the Name of Jesus!"

The words themselves are not important. The more technical you get the less power you will operate in because you are depending on 'the right words' instead of exercising faith in God. However, the manner in which you speak is important. Be earnest, wholehearted. There is no spiritual connection between volume level and spiritual impact. Demons don't have ear drums and people do, so you don't need to be loud. But you need to be bold, strong, and fervent. Take charge of the situation. Exert the authority of Jesus Christ and release the power of God when you speak.

Some people don't naturally take charge. They pray really sweet prayers. While sweet prayers work just fine for your relationship with God, you are going to have to hit your "Rambo" button and let "Mama bear" or "Papa bear" do some serious violence to the powers of darkness. Imagine a bully picking on your child at the playground. You may start off, "Would you please stop?" but if the bully persists, you get strong and say, "Hey! Cut it out now!" You can't appeal to the "kindness" of demons. You have to rise up, tap into your "inner-Rambo" and take over in the authority and power of Jesus Christ!

*"The **effectual fervent** prayer of a righteous man **availeth much**."* (Jms. 5:16, KJV)

Jesus often healed people by commanding people to do something they couldn't do before. We would also periodically have Anya do something she couldn't do before. In her case, we would have her walk. For someone else, it may be to reach their hand up if they had a shoulder problem, or touch their toes if they had a back issue, or to read a business card if they had eye problems. Some people can't do anything to immediately test their change, but change will become apparent over time.

WHAT'S THAT IN YOUR HAND?

When Moses was sent to Egypt to deliver the children of Israel, he told God, "They won't believe me." To remedy the situation, God gave Moses signs to perform. "The LORD said to him, "What is that in your hand?" (Ex. 4:2) Starting with what Moses already had, God equipped Moses to demonstrate signs and wonders. God says the same thing to us today. Do you know what you have in your hand already?

When Jesus sent the disciples out to proclaim the gospel, He said that those who believed the message that the apostles proclaimed would have supernatural signs that followed them.

*And he said to them, "Go into all the world and proclaim the gospel to the whole creation… And **these signs will accompany those who believe**: in my name they will cast out demons; they will speak in new tongues…**they will lay their hands on the sick, and they will recover**."* (Mark 16:15-18)

Did you see that Jesus Christ said that these signs would accompany ***those who believed*** the apostles message, not just the apostles? Are you casting out demons in the Name of Jesus, speaking with new tongues, and laying hands on the sick and seeing them recover? If not, you may have not received the full message that the apostles were sent out to proclaim.

The gospel that the apostles were sent to proclaim throughout the world was not merely a message about going to heaven when we die. Jesus came proclaiming, "The Kingdom of heaven is at hand." Jesus sent His disciples out with the proclamation that heaven has invaded earth to destroy the powers of hell and set the captives free. The proclamation was always accompanied with demonstrations of healing and deliverance. They were sent with the good news that God's 'sneak attack' on the devil was a glowing success! Jesus Christ had won the victory over sin, evil, disease, and even death itself on behalf of the entire human race. Now whosoever will repent and believe the good news will be forgiven, empowered by the gift of the Holy Spirit, and given the very authority of the Name of Jesus Christ to enforce His victory over devils, evil and disease. "In *My name they* **will** *cast out demons; they* **will** *speak in new tongues...* **they will lay their hands on the sick, and they will recover."** (Mark 16:15-18)

Jesus often healed with the touch of His hand.

> *And* **Jesus stretched out his hand and touched him**, *saying, "I will; be clean." And immediately his leprosy was cleansed.* (Matt. 8:3)

> **He touched her hand,** *and the fever left her, and she rose and began to serve him.* (Matt. 8:15)

> *But when the crowd had been put outside,* **he went in and took her by the hand**, *and the girl arose.* (Matt. 9:25)

The apostles and the early church followed this practice of healing by the laying on of hands.

> *And* **he took him by the right hand and raised him up**, *and immediately his feet and ankles were made strong.* (Act 3:7)

*Now many signs and wonders were regularly done among the people **by the hands** of the apostles* (Act 5:12)

*So Ananias departed and entered the house. And **laying his hands on him** he said, "Brother Saul, the Lord Jesus who appeared to you on the road by which you came has sent me so that you may **regain your sight and be filled with the Holy Spirit**."* (Act 9:17)

*And God was doing extraordinary miracles **by the hands** of Paul,* (Act 19:11)

What's that in your hand?   Perfect health is in your hand.

And his name—by faith in his name—has made this man strong whom you see and know, and the faith that is through Jesus has given the man this perfect health in the presence of you all. (Act 3:16)

The power that raised Jesus from the dead is in your hand to give life to mortal bodies.

If the Spirit of him who raised Jesus from the dead dwells in you, he who raised Christ Jesus from the dead will also give life to your mortal bodies through his Spirit who dwells in you. (Rom 8:11)

I've trained all kinds of Christians, from seminary trained pastors, to young children and illiterate villagers in third world countries, how to heal the sick with results in less than a few minutes by simply teaching them about what God says about their hand. It's not complicated. It's very simple!

Let me teach you about your hand. Take a look at your hand and say this, "This hand is not my hand. I am a member of the body of Jesus Christ. This hand belongs to Jesus Christ, the King of Kings and Lord of Lords! When I lay hands on the sick, the Kingdom of God is at hand! Jesus Christ is touching the sick with this hand. The power of the Spirit of God flows through me. Rivers of living water flow out through my inmost being. The

Spirit that raised Jesus Christ from the dead dwells inside of me. The power of Jesus Christ flows through me, to heal sickness, to heal disease, to impart healing, to restore bodies to life and perfect wholeness. I am a believer in Jesus Christ and His victory over all the power of evil. I never stop believing. When I lay hands on the sick, they shall recover, in Jesus' Name."

When I minister healing, I will usually lay my hand on the person believing that God's power flows through me. Think of your hand as a spiritual jumper cable or an extension cord from heaven that transmits the power of the Holy Spirit. Sometimes I'll just take their hand in mine like holding a handshake. Other times I'll place my hand on the area that needs to be healed. Sometimes with children, I've found it works well to allow young children to sit on my lap while they face their mommy or daddy. There is no particular 'right way.' Simply believe Jesus Christ for healing, but as you do, remember that Jesus Christ lives inside of you and His Spirit flows through your touch to crush sickness and disease and impart healing virtue into others.

"What happens if nothing happens?" is a question I often get. First, something is always happening. You are releasing the power of God in the authority of the Kingdom. God is working. Believe His word, not your eyes. Eventually you will see change with your eyes if you persevere in faith. Second, if the change that Jesus purchased hasn't fully manifested, we persist until it does manifest. Jesus had to pray twice for a blind man to receive full recovery. I'm sure it's okay for us to continue to address situations as often as required until they change.

Our team persisted for 30 minutes before we saw change in Anya. When we would ask Anya to walk, when we would see no apparent change, it was not as if we would begin to think to ourselves, "That didn't work. Let's try again." In our minds, Anya was already healed and we were simply pouring in more healing virtue until her healing manifested.

When a patient gets a shot from the doctor to cure a disease, if they look at the doctor just after they just received the shot and say, "I still don't feel any better. I don't think that worked" the doctor just responds by saying,

"You'll be fine in no time. The medicine is working. Just be patient." God's power is at work. We can continue to release more and more of the life of Christ until we see healing manifest.

Although we are believing God for complete healing each time we lay hands on anyone, at this point, as you will read in the next section, our team is seeing progressive healings. Significant changes are taking place, but it often seems like every inch must be won through a fight. However, once you've seen that it's God's will to heal your child, that Jesus Christ has already paid for it, and that God's given you the power and authority to impart to your child all that they need from God, you can never pretend like you don't know God. Faith and love isn't something that we try to "see if it works." It's the only way to live. It's the way of Jesus Christ.

As we conclude section one, I want to summarize a few simple elements that you can use to minister healing to your loved ones. Whether they are afflicted with birth defects or a sore neck, the process is the same.

1) Lay hands on the sick. Believe that the power of the Spirit of Jesus Christ flows out of you to heal the sick. You are the body of Christ. When your hand touches your child, Jesus Christ is laying hands on the sick.

2) Declare the Word of God and command everything to come into line with the will of God. Command that the devil and all his affliction depart. Command the body to be completely healed and whole in the Name of Jesus. Declare the victory and provision of Jesus Christ for healing.

3) Believe you have received everything the Word of God says you have received. You've already received victory over all evil. By His stripes, you are already healed. Thank God for what you've already received through Jesus Christ.

4) Expect changes. If possible, have them do something they could not do before to test their healing. Start keeping a journal of changes you are seeing through the power of God.

5) Don't give any place to doubt or ever speak a word contrary to what God says in His Word. It's inevitable that doubts arise because the flesh is constantly warring against the Spirit. Just don't take them to heart. Fill your heart and your mouth with the Word of God.

6) Persevere and persist without wavering. Keep your eyes fixed and your heart grounded in the victory we have in Jesus.

"Do not be sluggish, but be imitators of those who **through faith and patience** *inherit the promises."* (Heb. 6:12)

"For the one who doubts is like a wave of the sea that is driven and tossed by the wind. For that person must not suppose that he will receive anything from the Lord; he is a double-minded man, unstable in all his ways." (James 1:6-8)

I strongly encourage you to make your highest priority to discover and enjoy your union with Jesus Christ in everything. Let this become the solid foundation of your life and a constant source of joy, *"for the joy of the Lord is your strength."* (Neh. 8:10) As you minister to your child regularly, declare war on birth defect and take charge of the situation in the authority and power of Jesus Christ. Rejoice daily that He's already finished the work that's required both to establish you in your union with Him and to heal the sick through you!

CHAPTER 7

TAKING HEALING TO THE STREETS

Religion and Jesus don't mix well. Jesus was killed by religious people. Religion uses accusation to keep everyone with the program, abiding by the traditions and sticking to the routine. Jesus uses power and truth to set people free and make them well. Religion is always looking for a reason to accuse people of a fault. Jesus is always looking for a way to show people how much God loves them even if it means violating standard protocol.

Jesus Christ did not come to bring the world a new religion. He brought us an alternative to religion. Religion thrives on "holy men", doing "holy things", in "holy buildings", standing between God and unholy people. Religions thrives on separation between people and God. Jesus came to make us all God's own holy priesthood, whose every word and deed is a "holy thing." We who believe in Jesus have become the very dwelling place of God on earth, God's own living, breathing Holy Temple. Jesus makes us carriers of the presence of God. No more separation! We don't need religious men, doing religious things in religious places to bring us close to God. Jesus is the way, the truth and the life, and through Him we come to the Father! We are free from religious systems because Jesus Christ has brought us into union with God.

Jesus did not come to bring us a new religion. Religion lives by dead rituals, traditions, dogma, and rules. It's all external, performance based and conformity driven. Jesus Christ brought new life, divine life on the inside. Jesus came to put God's life inside of us to flow out from us, spontaneously, continuously, and creatively. Adam and Eve were not in the garden lighting candles, burning incense, studying theology, and developing religious organization charts. They weren't created for religion. They walked with God together. God walked with them. They were created for fellowship. Jesus walked with us too. Why? Jesus did not bring us religion. He brought relationship. He loved us. He walked with us. Religion doesn't know how to love. Religion destroys love. Religion killed Jesus Christ, God in the flesh, the true and living God who *is love*. Jesus brought us the love of God. Jesus came to bring people into a new relationship, to know God as their own Father, to bring people into their true destiny to walk with God as His very own sons.

Jesus did not bring us into a new religion. Jesus came with a "government upon His shoulders", the reign of the Kingdom of Heaven. He came to bring us into a new Kingdom, the Kingdom of God that sets men free. Jesus Christ brings people divine life from the Father that governs us and sets us free to live as sons of God. As Rom 5:17 says, "Those who receive the abundance of grace and the free gift of righteousness **reign in life** through the one man Jesus Christ." Religion doesn't give people righteousness. Religion doesn't give people grace. It give's rules and guilt. Allowing religion to govern someone's life never empowers people to reign in divine life. It makes everyone a slave to serve a dead system. It was the religious people, who didn't like God's government setting people free from their system, that killed Jesus. It still kills today. Jesus came to give us life, a life that reigns in us and empowers us to reign.

> *Jesus did not come to bring us a new religion. He came to bring us an alternative to religion.*

Religion comes with rules, traditions, hierarchy, creeds and expectations. It comes with words to conform, to recruit, to argue, to manage, to accuse, to manipulate, and if that doesn't work… words to kill. Jesus came with words too, but His words were "Spirit and Life." His words give grace. His words unleashed an encounter with a living person, the Spirit of Life. Even though Jesus used words to minister to others, His words were never mere words. He came with demonstration and power. He healed the sick, cast out demons, and raised the dead… with *words*! Religion conducts funerals. Jesus raises the dead. Those who live in Christ are learning to minister with words and demonstration today, with words of life that demonstrate the power of God by healing the sick, casting out demons, and even raising the dead.

HEALING IS SUPER ~~NATURAL~~ NORMAL

Healing is normal Christianity for all believers. We heal the sick not because we are super spiritual. We heal the sick because the Kingdom of God is near and we are under orders from heaven. The sick are healed because Jesus is King and we minister in His Name, not as a sign of our own spirituality. Healing indicates NOTHING about our spiritual status. Healing is a sign of the victory, compassion, and presence of Jesus Christ.

You may still have some questions regarding whether healing is for today, or whether healing is for you, or how God can use you to heal the sick. Here is my encouragement. In addition to continuing to search the Scriptures for the heart of God and revelation of Christ in this matter, I would like to appeal to you to set your doubts aside and focus on *acting on what you do understand* and *do believe* instead of whatever has you confused! Jesus said, "**Go** and learn what this means. God desires mercy…" Jesus wasn't

> *Healing the sick is normal Christianity for all believers, because healing the sick is normal for Jesus Christ who lives inside of them.*

sending the Pharisees off to do more Bible study. He was sending them off to go and learn mercy, to go and find some people who need the mercy of God and help them until the mercy of God enters their hearts. Often the path becomes clearer as we walk further down the road, "leaning not on our own understanding, acknowledging Him in all our ways…" So get out there and help some hurting people!

When I first came into this revelation regarding God's will to heal the sick through believers today, I had quite a few "theological loose ends." At that time, I still didn't know what to make of "Timothy's stomach."[2] Nor was I able to answer every objection that my fellow believers brought up to me. In the beginning, I didn't even see many instant healings either, but I decided *not* to base my faith on my experience or my doubts. I decided to live out my faith in Christ based on what I did see and understood clearly-

---

[2] **see** FAQ #1

that Jesus Christ is the Lord who lives in me to do His works through me, which includes healing the sick. It's always been part of His work.

Had I decided to wait until I had every Bible verse wrapped up in irrefutable clarity, I'd still be studying… and helping no one. Had I decided to stop the first time that someone I ministered to was not healed, there would be countless people dead, sick, and debilitated who are now still alive and well.

Will you be like Peter and step out of the boat with your eyes fixed on Jesus even though it defies your experience and He remains in the distance, almost ghostlike? Or will you be like Peter and sink, because you fixed your eyes on the waves, your past experiences, your personal fears, opposition from those you love, and your doubts? You must decide.

You wouldn't be reading this book this far if you were someone who wasn't ready to walk this out. So the remainder of this chapter will be focused on equipping you to "walk on water" in healing the sick to demonstrate the Kingdom and reach people for Jesus Christ and equip them to walk in His fullness as His disciples

PRACTICAL HEALING MINISTRY

In the remainder of this chapter, I'd like to give you some practical guidance about ways you can demonstrate the power of God as part of your Kingdom lifestyle. As I do so, please understand, ministry is *never* a formula or a method. However, God seems to know that we need models, demonstration and examples to move forward to release God's kingdom in our lives. This is why God not only gave us His Word, but also those who are called to equip the body of Christ by being examples and sharing what they have learned.

Consider the following pointers as a starting place to help get you going. You will eventually develop you own approaches as you walk with God and have your own experiences. So don't worry about "doing the formula" or "following the method." Follow Jesus Christ and stay flexible.

Here is an overview of a general flow I've experienced in ministering the power of God with strangers in public:

1. Approach
2. Ask
3. Minister
4. Test
5. Rejoice or Repeat
6. Connect and Close

1. **Approach**: Go to people. Build rapport quickly with a pleasant demeanor. Take as much time to building rapport as you feel is appropriate or necessary.

2. **Ask:** Say something like, "I noticed you were walking with a cane and thought, you're too young and good looking to be using a cane. What happened? Do you have pain?" Or, if there is no visible condition like a cane, crutch, or an oxygen tank, you can say, "This may sound crazy, but I was wondering if you have anything that causes pain in your body? I have a special gift to be able to set people free from pain and I just felt like I should ask you."

3. **Minister:** Tell them. "I can help you with that. Are you ready for that pain to go?" While holding out your hand like you're asking for money, say "Let me see your hand for a second" They'll put their hand in yours automatically, even if they are wondering what you are about to do. Then grasp their hand firmly (but not hard enough to hurt them), and minister healing, "Father, thank you for all you've done. In Jesus' Name, pain/sickness, Go now. Be healed. I set you free in Jesus' Name"

4. **Test:** Then immediately say, "Now test that out. Move it around and tell me what's changed."

   Testing Tips:
   - Make up your mind from the beginning that you will have people test their condition. It's often the *action of faith* that activates the working of miracles. Tell people, "Do something you couldn't do. Tell me what's changed." In sports, when someone

throws, hits, or kicks a ball, everyone understands that power is released in the *follow through*. Miracles are the same way. Usually, when people are not seeing results in public it's because they are still working through their personal insecurities and are relieved to finally get a chance to pray for someone. When you act on your faith by having them test their condition, it releases more of God's power than when you "pull your punches" and minister with no follow through.

- Quantify Pain Level: If they have pain, ask them to tell you the level of their pain on a scale of 1 to ten. I usually say, "So what level is your pain right now on a scale of 1 to 10. 10 is like having a baby and 1 is like someone standing on your toe." After you minister, have them move it and tell you what the pain level is now. It's more encouraging to hear "It was an 8 and now it's a 2," than it is to hear, "Nope. It's still there." Helping people quantify their pain level from the outset can help you both recognize the progressive miracles of God.

- *Never* give medical advice. Some medical conditions are not immediately testable, such as diabetes or A.I.D.S. Others only experience the symptoms of their conditions when they stop taking medication. Understand that in most modern countries it is illegal to ever give anyone medical advice or tell them to go against directives given by their doctors. Simply encourage them to expect their healing to manifest. Even if they ask you explicitly, "Do you think I should stop taking my medicine?" I just say, "That's not my business. You need to make those decisions for yourself. There's no pill big enough that can stop God from healing you." Leave their medical decisions between them, God, and their doctors.

5. **Rejoice or Repeat:** Rejoice in their healing or Repeat the process, by saying, "Sometimes I pray more than once. Let's hit this again quickly." Then take their hands and command healing once more.

Here are a few recommendations for repeating the healing ministry in public:

- STAY WITH THE SAME APPROACH. When you start to change your approach, generally you are starting to operate in the power of the mind instead of the authority of the Spirit. Going on a search for the right words or correct diagnosis tends to get you out of the Spirit and into your mind which ultimately hinders the release of power. Just fix your eyes upon Jesus Christ, His absolute victory through the finished work of the cross, and give it another blast. If anything, I encourage you to be more general and less specific with your words and more focused on releasing the power of the Holy Spirit. "I said Go NOW. Be completely healed in the Name of Jesus. Now, move it again. What's changed? Still the same. Then once more, in Jesus' Name, BE HEALED. Move it now."

- KEEP YOUR PRAYERS BRIEF so you can TEST FREQUENTLY. If you pray for two minutes your first time around, guess how many opportunities to pray twice you'll have with a stranger? Probably not very many. So keep your hands-on ministry brief and test often. You can get 20 whacks at something in less than 5 minutes when you keep your ministry simple. "Boom! How's that? Boom! How about now? Boom! Need some more?" Remember, we're not heard because of our many words. We're releasing the finished work of Jesus Christ. Jesus Christ has placed the loaded gun in our hands. Now, just release power that's in your hand. Just draw the gun, pull the trigger, and check the target. If you need to, fire again! You don't need to proclaim the assembly instructions for the gun or go online to purchase bullets.

6) Connect and Close: When it's time to wrap up your spontaneous healing ministry, you will have experienced one of three results:

1) They have not noticed any change

2) They have experienced some improvement but are not yet completely healed

3) They are completely healed.

Let's go through some tips about how to handle each of these different scenarios. We'll hit the most challenging scenario first, and the others are simple.

"What do you do when you minister to someone and nothing happens?" This is the scary "Goliath" scenario that the enemy tries to use to keep the church of God intimidated into doing nothing. But I've found that it's not very scary at all, especially once you forget about you and stop looking to ministry results to affirm your standing with God. Base your standing with God on your union with Jesus Christ and allow ministry to become an overflow of His love and victory to others.

When it comes to wrapping up ministry that had no *apparent* results, here are a few things to consider:

- They were already NOT healed before you met them. Now they are not yet healed, but LOVED IN THE NAME OF JESUS.

- Just because they didn't experience change immediately, doesn't mean that they aren't healed. You just released God's healing power into them. Once a doctor gives a patient a shot, he doesn't worry about the patients current symptoms any longer because he realizes the medicine will work. We have the most potent medicine in the universe!

- Your actions of obedience are worship to Jesus and love to your fellow man. Stepping out in faith is sowing to the Spirit, which will bring a harvest. Be of good courage. Keep laying hands, worshipping Jesus, agreeing with heaven, and you will see a harvest!

- Everyone wants the power to manifest miracles instantly consistently flowing from their lives. But sticking your neck out over and over and allowing the Lord to do His work in you is the path to get there! Keep walking forward! Challenge yourself to do the things that build up your life in the spirit like communion with God in the Word, confessing the Scriptures, praying in tongues, singing worship songs, or whatever else builds you up spiritually.

- The heavens and the earth are watching you. God, demons and angels watch your life more than your results. So do people of whom you may not even be aware. Several times I've had people come to me, not because they saw someone get out of a wheelchair, but because they saw me laying hands on someone in a wheelchair. (You do draw *more* when they see people get out of wheelchairs, but still…)

- The alternative (i.e. doing nothing for hurting people that Jesus loves when you could do something) doesn't fit the Spirit of God in you. It's not acceptable to you, much less to God. So put it out of your mind as an option. Don't play multiple choice. Put yourself on spiritual "auto-pilot" and condition yourself to automatically move towards the needs you see around you without evaluating the situation any further: I see. BOOM, I act. It's a reflex of love.

- Nothing NEVER happens… unless you actually decided to do nothing. If you try… SOMETHING good happened. You stepped out in faith and love and released the Kingdom. Awesome! Now, don't pull your faith back based on what your eyes see. Don't unplug your faith and default to disbelief. You've opened heaven's door to flow with power. Keep it open. Give God time. If you need to, you can pray again. If you don't quit and get discouraged, you'll see Jesus' results.

With those pointers in mind, when it seems like my new friend is getting ready to move on, here's how I often wrap up a spontaneous ministry session with a stranger, "Thank you so much for allowing me to pray for you. I know God loves you and wants you well and with Him forever. He paid an awesome price for you when Jesus died on the cross. (IF they aren't yet completely healed…) I'm believing God for complete recovery in your body. Or (IF they are healed) I'm so glad you were able to receive what He purchased for you. I'm happy I had a chance to meet you. You are so worth it. Look, here's my card with my contact information. If you ever need anything, please give me a call." Shake their hand and walk away praising and thanking Jesus for the victory He's won for them and the privilege it is to know Him and exercise His dominion on the earth.

Even if they've not yet experienced change in their body, and often if they have received healing, there may be grace to go further with the interaction and speak into their lives. If not, WRAP IT UP. But in the case where there is grace to carry the interaction further I'll often say something like this, "You know I think that God wants you to understand something. You can never look at the condition of your body or the circumstances in your life and to see the whole truth about His love for you. God demonstrates His love for you in what happened to the body of His Son. He joined the human race to live and die for you because you are so precious to Him. He rose again and is alive now to give you victory over everything that defeats you. Do you know Him? Is Jesus Christ your Lord?" Then see what happens.

ENCOURAGEMENT FROM "SLOW MIRACLES"

One afternoon I took my family to a small traveling fair in a local parking lot. As we walked around I noticed a man pulling an oxygen tank. As it turned out, it was an acquaintance of mine from years back named Isaac. Isaac was a large, tall, light skinned African American man, but when I saw him today his skin was almost yellow. I asked him what was going on and he told me, "I've got C.O.P.D. They've put me on hospice and say I've only got a couple of months, so I wanted to bring my son out to the fair today." I said, "Well that's not right! I want to pray for your healing right now." I reached my hand and put it on his chest. I said, "Right now, in the Name of Jesus, I command COPD to leave him. Lungs, be restored and healed, now! Now, Isaac, take a deep breath and tell me what's happening." He took a big breath… "Cough, hack, wheeze." So I said, "Don't worry. I'm going to hit this again, because it has to go. In the Name of Jesus, lungs you be healed and restored. All COPD leave him now. Take another deep breath Isaac." Isaac breathed in… "Wheeze, cough, hack." It still hadn't left.

At this point, Isaac was ready to move on with his day at the fair with his son. He said, "Thanks for trying." So I closed up the interaction by saying, "I'm not trying. I'm believing God for your complete recovery. Jesus said, "Believers will lay hands on the sick and they shall recover" so I'm believing you'll be completely restored. Great to see you man. Have a great rest of the day with your son!"

One year later, my wife and I were coming out of Walmart and I noticed a man on the bench just outside the store with a chrome four-pronged cane. So I walked over to him and was surprised to see Isaac sitting there with no oxygen tank and great color. I said, "Isaac! How are you doing man? Where's your oxygen tank?" Isaac exhaled a big puff of his cigarette and said, "Don't need them no more. Jesus healed me!" Wow!

So I asked him about his cane, and he said that he had a bad back and shooting pain through his hip and leg. I said, "Now if Jesus was able to heal your C.O.P.D., do you think He can heal your back and hip?" I laid hands on Isaac and had him test it. He stood up with no pain and walked with no pain. But I noticed a little too much swagger in his stride. So I asked if we could check his alignment. He sat back straight on the bench and I held his legs up in front of him. One of his legs was a clear half inch shorter than the other. So I told him to watch his feet and said, "In the Name of Jesus, short leg grow. Perfect alignment now." His leg immediately shot out until it was even with the other.

I said, "Check it now." Isaac stood up and began walking with a nice, even stride and no pain at all. He bent over, twisted around... still no pain! Out of habit though, he still had his cane in his hand as he walked, but was not using it at all. I told him, "I don't think you'll be needing that cane anymore." Isaac, then lifted the cane above his head, and began saying, "Yah. I don't need this no more!" Then he started to get louder, pumping the cane up and down over his head, "Hey, I don't need this no more. Jesus done healed me!" In his excitement, he started shouting and pumping his cane above his head.

The sight of a large man swinging a metal bar above his head and shouting in front of Walmart began to gather some on lookers. Some were afraid to come too close and were pausing on their way in, while others did the same thing on their way out. And here's Isaac, still shouting, "Jesus just healed me! I'm healed! I don't need this cane no more" So I joined in the fun and said, "I just prayed for my friend Isaac, and God healed his back... while he was smoking a cigarette! So I want you to know that Jesus is real. He loves you. He's ready to take you as you are and change your life. Is there anyone here that has any pain or sickness in your body? I want to pray for you right now, real quick and Jesus will heal you too! Don't worry about what you believe or how you think you've been living. This isn't a religious thing.

This is about God's love for you. So if you have pain or sickness we want to pray for you real quick. Who has pain or sickness? Anything at all?" Then the Kingdom ministry continued for another 20 minutes right in front of Walmart.

EARS TO HEAR

On a recent mission trip, while walking to the market from my hotel, a young Muslim man began to speak to us in English. He was a seaman by trade but was in port for several weeks. We spoke for a while, so before I left I asked him if he had anything that gave him any pain or problems in his health. He told me that he was very concerned about his ear. Eight weeks earlier he suddenly lost his hearing in his ear. He had no idea what had happened and was very concerned that he would be deaf in his ear the rest of his life. I told him that I had seen God heal many people through my prayers, and I would like to lay my hand on his ear to pray for his hearing to be restored. He agreed. Three times I said, "In the Name of Jesus Christ, you deaf spirit, come out now. Ear, be healed and whole. Hear." But each time we checked, he said, "I'm sorry. It is still the same." So after the third time, I wrapped up the interaction by telling him that I will continue to believe that God will heal his ear quickly.

There was a large part of me that was tempted to be disappointed. After all, this had been an obvious "divine appointment" with an English speaking Muslim who was open to experiencing the power of God in Jesus Christ. I stepped out, laid hands expecting a miracle and nothing perceptible happened. But I knew better than to agree with the temptation to be disappointed. Instead, I stirred myself to rejoice in the Lord and give thanks to Him. "Thank you Jesus for the privilege of representing heaven on the earth. Thank You that you are faithful to stand by the gospel with your power and signs follow me wherever I go. Thank you for opening the door for this ministry. Thank you that believers will lay hands on the sick and they will recover. I thank You in advance that this man will recover his hearing."

Two days later, I was walking again in the same part of town and I heard someone behind me calling my name. It was this same man. He was jogging up towards me with a big smile. "Mr. Andrew. My ear. It is well now! It is well! I woke the next morning after you had prayed and it was well."

"Completely?" I asked. He said, "Yes. It is perfect." So we had a nice little chat about how God showed His love for us in Jesus Christ.

Many times at the close of a service, after I've prayed for people with little obvious results, they come find me the next day to tell me they are healed. One lady had her tail bone surgically removed because of an auto accident. She was in constant pain and asked for prayer for the pain. That night, the pain went away, but the next day she came to me and said, "It grew back last night. I have a tail bone again!"

Another lady had chronic pain in her hips and legs that was hindering her ability to care for her family and do her job. I ministered to her for a number of minutes and only saw her pain reduce. However, she came in the next day with no pain. Months later she is still pain free!

In another instance, I was asked by a friend to come to the hospital to minister to his father. His father had been battling leukemia for years but wasn't a believer. He had contracted a disease that had caused large legions to grow in his throat that made it impossible for him to eat or even to swallow water. The doctors were getting worried because they had given him several courses of the strongest antibiotic possible, and it had only gotten worse. At his son's persuasion, he finally agreed to let me come and pray for him, figuring that he didn't have anything to lose. So I laid hands on him and asked him to give me a report, telling him that I'd be happy to come and pray again if need be.

I didn't hear anything the next day or the next. Whenever I would wonder about my friend's dad, I would hear this thought, "The reason they haven't called you is because nothing happened. They are probably planning his funeral. Blah, blah, blah." I didn't agree with those thoughts, but they were there. Several months later I heard from my friend again. He wanted me to pray for his sister. So I asked him, "How is your father?" My friend said, "Oh, I've been meaning to tell you. The next morning, my father woke up and ate a full breakfast and checked out of the hospital that afternoon. He was completely healed. The doctors were amazed. In fact, since then his leukemia numbers have made a huge swing and are better than they've ever been and are still making progress."

I share these experiences not to discourage you from believing God for instant miracles, but to encourage you to believe God for miracles even if they don't happen instantly.

MISPLACING OUR IDENTITY IN MIRACLES
One afternoon, several of my friends set aside some time together to go into the city to touch people with the love of the Kingdom. After we were finished, we gathered back at our house for some pizza and fellowship. I was sent to the grocery store to pick up some drinks and paper plates.

One of the young ladies who had gone out with another group asked if she could come with me. As we walked through the store, I saw a few people that needed ministry, so I started conversations and asked them if my friend could pray for them. After she prayed for the third person, she looked at me and said, "I must be some sort of jinx or something!" I said, "Huh?" She continued, "I just mean that I'm not seeing miracles, and I want to see miracles!" Although I was excited about her zeal, I felt compelled to address something. I said, "First of all, you are not a jinx. You are a daughter of the living God and an ambassador of His Kingdom. Second, stop trying to get your identity from your ministry results. We don't need miracles to happen to make ourselves feel affirmed. We want miracles for the people who are hurting and for the glory of God."

We turned to go and check out and hadn't walked more than ten steps when I saw a lady who was bent over pushing a shopping cart with a walker inside of it. Her husband was with her so I decided to speak to her husband first. I said, "How are you today? I noticed your wife's walker. Is she in pain?" He told me a little about his wife's condition. Then I said, "Wow! Today is your lucky day! My friends and I have a ministry of praying for people and seeing them healed. Can we pray real quick?" He responded, "Well my hip is in terrible pain." I said, "Great. Then I'll pray for you and my friend can pray for your wife."

As we asked a little more, the wife said, "Not only do I have pain in my back, my bones are a mess. So this is actually as far up as I can go." While I ministered to the husband, my friend, who had just called herself a jinx, laid hands on this lady. The husband said, "It's gone!" He was healed. Then the lady said, "I felt something when you prayed!" She wasn't healed yet, so my friend prayed a second time. This time my friend said, "Can you feel that?" The lady stood up straight and said, "My bones! Oh my, this is strange!" She was completely healed. God had healed her back through my friend.

When we go after miracles so we can affirm our own sense of identity, we get it backwards. We don't get our identity from doing miracles. Miracles come from our identity! We don't look to miracles to tell us that we are children of God. The word of God tells us that! We don't heal so that we can prove ourselves. We are free from all that. Our identity is established in the unshakable union we have with Jesus Christ. As we walk in this, God's power and love flows through us and people are blessed.

I have had many other instances of people experiencing no apparent change at the moment of ministry who returned later to say, "Do you remember when you prayed for me? Well, later that night I noticed I had no more pain. I've been better ever since then!" The more you step out, you'll begin to have these same kind experiences. So relax. Love people. Believe heaven for healing. Expect miracles, but if no instant miracle takes place, expect recovery.

CHAPTER 8

DEVLOPING A KINGDOM LIFESTYLE

Healing the sick and walking in the power of the Kingdom can be part of your everyday lifestyle. While I believe that it can be important to set aside some time specifically to go out to minister to people in the Name of Jesus, it's more important that this become part of your everyday life. Many people have a fairly full schedule, so it's important NOT to relegate Kingdom ministry to a couple hours on an outreach once a week. Go ahead and schedule some special outreaches, but look for ways to incorporate this into things you are already doing.

Here are some practical pointers to get you started healing the sick as a lifestyle:

1) **Shopping**- Whenever you interact with employees of businesses that you patronize (e.g. store cashiers, floor workers, waitresses/waiters of restaurants, bank tellers, and other service oriented positions) you can ask them if they have any pain from standing around. "How are you doing today? You're working hard and on your feet. Do you have anything that gives you pain, like your feet or back?" If they have pain, just hold your hand out towards them and ask them, "Give me your hand real quick. I can help you." Once they put their hand in yours, just say, "I'm going to pray real quickly, and God will heal you. In the Name of Jesus, all pain go, be completely healed. Move it now and tell me what's happened."

My youngest daughter, Phoebe, was seven years old when she started to walk in the power of God. There was one evening that she was in our van with Tina when she stopped to get some gas. Tina asked, "Do you want to wait in the van or come in while I go pay?" Phoebe paused and said, "I'm coming in. Someone needs prayer in there." So they went in and there was no one in the entire store except for the cashier. Phoebe walked up to the cashier and said, "Hi! Do you have any pain in your body?" The surprised cashier said, "Well how sweet! Yes, I've got a bad back from an accident. It always hurts." Phoebe said, "Let me see your hand, I want to pray for you." The cashier gives her hand to Phoebe and says, "You are so sweet!" Then Phoebe says, "In the Name of Jesus and the power of the Holy Spirit, all pain, you leave her now. Back be healed! Now, move around!" The cashier stood there a little dumbfounded now and said to Phoebe, "You are so cute!" Phoebe looked right back at her and said, "This isn't cute! Move around and try your back." (Yes, she is very definitely on the spunky side.) Then the cashier moved and her jaw dropped, "O my God! Little girl, what did you just do?" Her back was healed. At this point my wife jumped in and shared Jesus with the cashier.

How often do you pass retail workers at cash registers, stocking shelves, organizing merchandize? There are so many people who are working in spite of pain in their body, because they have to. They are doing their best to get through each day with great pain. You can be God's instrument to encounter them with the Kingdom of God.

When you're at a store and need help finding something, before the floor worker takes off, you can say "You're on your feet a lot with this job, aren't you? Do you have anything that gives you pain from standing or moving?" When they tell you about their pain, just hold out your hand, and say, "Let me help you with that. Let me see your hand for a second." If you're holding out your hand (as if asking for money or checking for rain drops) they'll put their hand in yours automatically. Grip it, and say, "Thank you Father for your love and power. In Jesus Name, all pain go now. Be restored." Then tell them, "Move it now and tell me what's changed."

Recently I was at a store and noticed a lady stocking one of the shelves. I approached her with a smile and said, "Hi!" She said, "Can I help you?" I said, "Well, I don't need any help, but I might be able to help you." She chuckled and said, "Really? How?" I said, "You have a pretty physical job. Do you have anything in your body giving you pain? Anything at all?" She said, "I'm supposed to get my knee replaced in a couple of weeks. It always hurts me. Why? Are you selling something?" I said, "No. I'm not selling anything, but I can take care of that knee replacement right now for free." She said, "You're kidding, right? How?" I said, "It's easier to show you than explain it. (I held out my hand and said...) Give me your hand real quickly." She put her hand in mine and I commanded that all pain leave and that her knee be made new and whole in Jesus' Name. I told her to move it and tell me how it felt and let me know what's different. Her face lit up, "All the pain is gone!" I told her to walk around and make sure. As she did this she said, "This is so strange. I don't even believe this stuff. Oh my, there is no pain." She was still smiling because the pain in her knee was gone. Then her face dropped with the realization that the God she didn't believe in just healed her knee in the Name of Jesus Christ. She looked at me and said, "Well, thank you." The "do not disturb" sign just went up. She was afraid of a sermon. So I gave her a brief hug and told her, "Jesus loves you so much! You have a great day!" and I left. I left her with a new knee, a hug, and the Name of Jesus!

God can use you to touch people wherever they are, even while you are shopping!

2) **Eating Out**- Whenever you are at a sit down restaurant, you can truly shine the light by being the most loving customer your table-server, hostesses, bus-boys, and managers has ever encountered! Build a relationship with your table-server. Ask them if they have any pain. You can also tell them, "We usually pray over our meal and we'd love to pray for you too. If God were to do a miracle in your life, what would it be?" You can follow this up by asking if they have any pain or anything for which they take medication, so that you can pray for their healing. You can also use your interactions as an opportunity to speak into their lives. There have been many times that God has brought our table-servers to tears and we've departed with hugs.

I remember one time that I had just gotten off the plane and we stopped at a restaurant for some lunch. We built some rapport with the waitress by asking her about her day and making some small talk. When she brought us our food, she asked, "Is there anything else I can get you?" I said, "Yes, one thing. We normally pray over our meals and we'd love to pray for you too. Do you have anything that gives you pain or problems physically? We've seen people healed." She paused and got a little flush, not quite sure what to say to such an unusual request, but then she said, "Well, actually I have constant back pain from an accident." So I asked her, "Give me your hand real quickly. I know you need to keep moving." She put her hand in mine, and I said, "In the name of Jesus I command all pain to come out of her. Back be healed." I told her, "Thanks. We don't want to slow you down darling. But you let me know how your back feels before we leave."

She left the table and went back to pick up some orders from the cooks. When she came out from behind the divider into the dining area, she had a tray with several plates of food on her shoulder. She was glowing and tears were coming from her eyes and she looked over at me and mouthed the word, "Thank you!" I knew she had been healed.

After a little while, she got a free moment and returned to our table. She confirmed that she had in fact been healed and filled us in on more of the back story. She had suffered chronic back pain since an automobile accident several years back and that day it had been particularly unbearable. She also was a believer in Christ but had not been walking with Him closely. She felt that God was ashamed of her and was unhappy with her because she had not been walking closely. But when she got healed, she knew that God still loved her and was inviting her to step back into His grace! Praise the Lord!

Before we leave the subject of table-servers… leave a good tip. Demonstrate the extravagant generosity of God with your tip! If you're not going to tip them well, go to a fast food restaurant or stay home. Unfortunately, Christians have earned the reputation of being terrible tippers. This ought not to be! Be generous, even extravagant, in Jesus' Name.

Another thing you can do to bless anyone who serves you in a restaurant, store or business, is to ask to see the manager. When the manager comes over, commend the service of your server to the manager. Often, managers only hear complaints. So if your server did a good job, take a little time to share that with the manager.

3) **Treat People like Friends, Not Strangers**. When you are out and about, you can start conversations with strangers by choosing to treat them like friends. Look for the obvious— people with crutches, canes, oxygen tanks, arm and knee braces, or limps. Take notice people who are moving in ways that indicate they are uncomfortable or are sitting on benches (because people who have pain or shortness of breath need extra rest). But don't forget the simple acts of taking notice of people who don't have any obvious needs. The warmth of your smile and kindness of you words can open the door for Jesus to flow into their

lives. While not everyone needs healing at a given time, everyone needs Jesus!

I was on a college campus once, and just wrapped up a really cool ministry encounter with a group of college students at the top of a set of stairs. As I walked down the stairs looking for another opportunity, I noticed a young with green hair, all sorts of nose, ear and lip piercings, who was slouched down in a chair. As I noticed him, he noticed me noticing him and turned away as if to indicate, "I'm not sure what you're doing but, whatever it is, I'm not interested."

Initially, I kept walking forward hoping to find someone else who seemed more receptive. No one was around. I looked down the sidewalk to my left. No one. I looked right. No one. Then I thought about the green haired man in the chair. I thought to myself, "I'm not sure how this is going to go, but I'm not about to let the threat of rejection keep me from obeying God. If he's going to reject me, I'm going to make him step up to the plate and do it. I'm not afraid. I don't need his acceptance. I'm going to give him God's acceptance. Let's go overcome evil with good!"

I turned around and walked right over to him. He now was in a conversation with a girl who had gotten off her bike to chat with him. He noticed me approaching, so with a smile from about ten feet away, I said, "Man. Cool hair! I noticed it from way over there. How long have you had it that color?" He said, "Oh, a few months." I followed up, "I'll bet you get a lot of comments." He smiled and said, "You got that right." So I pulled off my hat to reveal my male patterned baldness and said, "I don't get too many comments on my hair anymore." We burst out laughing together.

From there, I just changed the subject, "Hey man, I don't mean to bother you or anything, but my buddy and I came out here today just to pray for people. We've seen God heal people instantly already today. So if you have anything that gives you sickness or pain in your body, or need a miracle, we'd love to pray for you real quick." He softened and said, "Honestly, I'm feeling pretty good physically, but do you pray for depression?" God had done it! He opened the door for the Kingdom!

I didn't really care for green hair, but I wasn't being fake. I decided to like green hair right then for the sake of the Kingdom! I asked some questions to take a personal interest in him, but I didn't carry on so long that it made him feel like a stranger was getting into his business. I also found an opening for some genuine humor. When you are able, genuine humor has an amazing way of making people feel relaxed with you. But more than any of these particular skills, the most important thing was God giving me the grace to be perfectly willing to go to someone who I thought might reject me with a heart filled with peace and acceptance. This is why it is so important to build yourself up in the Spirit through faith in the gospel. When you are filled with God's grace, it comes out of you!

One of my favorite ways to approach strangers is to walk up to a group of people. With an enthusiastic demeanor, I say, "Hey! Would you like to see something cool?" This works especially well with younger adults and teen agers. They tend to be bored with life and always open to something to break up the monotony.

Usually, people will say, "Sure." So I continue, "Okay. So which of you have something that gives you pain, like an injury that didn't heal, or anything else that causes you problems? You'll love this." When you ask this question, watch people's eyes. Even if they hesitate to say anything, everyone will begin to look at the person they know complains the most. They'll often volunteer their friend for this "experiment".

Once I had a group of people with me that wanted to experience how I minister to people on the streets. I had them hang back about ten feet or so while I approached a group of five young people. After I asked which of them had pain, everyone turned towards the tallest young man. Then he said, "I've got a messed up shoulder. I've had three tours of duty in the Army and messed up my shoulder real bad." So I said, "Okay this is going to be awesome! Let me introduce my friends to you, because God uses them for miracles." As I brought the group over, one of them took the initiative to minister to the man with the hurt shoulder. He laid hands and the man's shoulder was instantly healed! We talked more to the group and several of them prayed to receive Jesus Christ as Lord and Savior right there.

On another occasion, I saw a couple of college aged guys coming out of a store in the mall. So I asked, "Hey guys! Do you want to see something cool?" They said, "Sure." "Which of you guys have something that gives you pain, like an injury that didn't heal right or anything like that?"

One of them said, "My hip is all f*#*#d up." I asked, "What happened?" He said, "I'm not sure. I was so drunk last night, I'm not sure what happened. But I've had surgery in the past, but I must have done something to f*#*# it up again." So I said, "Okay. Do this for me. Put your hand on your hip and I'm going to put my hand on your shoulder." I put my hand on his shoulder and left it there for about ten seconds saying nothing at all. I merely believed God for the power of Jesus to flow into his hip and heal the damage.

After about ten seconds, I took my hand off his shoulder and said, "Move it around now and see what's happened." He began to move and started dropping more F-bombs. After he settled down a little, I asked, "So do you know how that happened? Would you like to know?" He said, "Yeah, what's going on? That's freaky." I said, "It's Jesus. He's real and He loves you. You see, Jesus said believers will lay hands on the sick and they will recover. I believe in Jesus, so He lives in me and His power can flow through me to heal you. But don't miss the point. You hurt yourself because you got drunk last night. You dropped three F-bombs in less than a minute. And Jesus *still* healed you! He's really real and willing to forgive you. What He did for your hip, He can do for your whole life. But for Him to do this, you've got to be willing to trust Him and follow Him." Immediately, the same guy that was dropping all the F-bombs, whose hip just got healed, started to well up with tears in his eyes. God had touched his hip through the healing and was now touching his heart through the gospel.

While it may be most comfortable for you to approach individuals, it can be very power to approach people in groups. This allows them to remain in their comfort zone and helps them feel a little more secure about being approached by a stranger. Believe it or not, it may also help you have some productive interactions with people who may have otherwise blown you off if they had been alone (but since they don't want all their friends to see them treat you like a jerk, they interact with you with more restraint). When God's Kingdom is manifest through healing, several people will be touched at the same time. In fact, new churches and moves of God can start quickly by winning groups of people to Jesus Christ at the same time instead of just one by one.

4) **Develop a *lifestyle* of Kingdom**. Wherever you are, you are *always* an Ambassador of Jesus Christ on God's mission to represent heaven and set the captives free. Stop going shopping. Go and make disciples and pick up some groceries while you're at it. Make conversation with employees and other customers. Seek to impact at least one person for the sake of the Kingdom *every time you leave your house*. If you go shopping, keep your eyes open for people who are walking with limps, canes, walkers, crutches, support braces, oxygen tanks, people sitting on benches while others shop, motorized shopping carts, pharmacy customers, and people in wheel chairs. Taking an extra 5 or 10 minutes in every shopping trip can make a huge difference for tons of people. Over the course of your lifetime, you may see hundreds or even thousands of people come to know Jesus Christ if you'd be willing to do this one thing.

Whenever you wake up or leave your home, declare yourself to be an ambassador of Jesus Christ. Declare open doors and divine appointments. Give yourself some extra time and purpose to move into people's lives for the sake of the Kingdom.

5) If you are involved in a church, tell you pastoral staff that you'd like to visit the sick and infirm that are connected to your congregation. Tell your Bible study or friends that you've been learning about healing and want them to call you if they are ever sick. If you're on the worship team, ask your team members if they need healing for anything in their body.

6) Find a way to connect with the poor. Soup kitchens and parks are places that the homeless often hang out. They often have pain and health issues. The power of God can restore not only their bodies, but their hope, dignity, and value.

7) Go where people are out in public, shopping malls, stores, parks, or other such places. Be available and start conversations. Make yourself available. Be as outgoing and engaging as you can so that you shine with love and encouragement to the people you see. Look for people you can talk to. See where it goes.

8) Go to low-income housing projects or apartments. "Hi, I'm your neighbor and I wanted to introduce myself. I'm here because I believe in free health care for everyone. Is there anyone here who has pain or is on medication?"

9) Find like-minded believers with whom you can partner in the ministry of healing the sick. Policemen have authority and power. The carry a badge and a gun. But they also call on one another for back up.

Among the very religious or anti-religious, I sometimes find that it works best if I don't **ask** people if I can pray for them. When you say "Can I pray for you?" it can set off all sorts of religious land mines planted by the enemy. They may want to argue or run away. This has nothing to do with you or your approach. It only shows that the enemy of our souls has been hard at work.

Instead, after we've talked about their pain or health condition, I'll sometimes say, "Would you like to be well?" Or "Would you like to get rid of that right now?" Then I hold out my hand and **tell** people, "Give me your hand for a second." After they put their hand in my hand, I grip and say, "I'm going to pray for you real quickly and God will heal you. " Then I minister healing. Sometimes, the way the interaction develops seems to require that you let them know *why* you want to talk to them. So instead of asking people, "Can I pray for you?" I have found that it often works better to *tell* them, "I want to pray for you. I believe God wants you well and He'll heal you right now."

PRACTICAL ADVICE TO MAKING FRIENDS WITH STRANGER

- Smile, be outgoing. Treat people like they are your friend already.

- Ask questions. Be a good listener.

- Seek to understand people without judging. Be curious and learn about them, their challenges, and their interests.

- Love people. Find their value and ways to express it.

- Develop a sense of humor. Humor can be very disarming and engaging.

- Pay attention to body language to respect their space. Use space and posture to help them be comfortable with your presence.

- Don't worry about rejection. Every rejection is increasing your eternal reward. Why fear what can only increase your eternal blessing? Rejection is bringing you one step closer to those people who are prepared by God to be receptive toward you and your ministry. Just dust your feet and keep going.

So begin to incorporate the power of God into your lifestyle, your routine activities, wherever you are and whatever you do. It can be important to set aside some times specifically to reach out to others with God's love and power, but focus on developing a supernatural lifestyle.

GOING AROUND WALLS
Sometimes people who have pain or need healing may resist your initial offer to minister to them, but with a little persistence, perhaps a brief testimony or two, sometimes you'll see a door open for ministry. For those who are just getting started, depending upon your personality type, pushing through resistance may be more difficult for you. Most people are very receptive to prayer right from the start. As you develop experience, you will also grow in boldness and wisdom that will make you more effective in opening doors even with people who may not be initially receptive. Often they are just leery of "strangers acting strange", so when you continue to persist with gentleness and love, these barriers can be overcome. Regardless, if you approach people with grace, love, and respect, you will still release the fragrance of Jesus Christ in their lives.

Here are a few common barriers and some suggestions you may want to experiment with:

"No thank you. I pray at my church."

- With an enthusiastic smile, "Alright! So you already believe this. I do too. I'm going to add my prayers too. Real quick, Father, thank you for this beautiful person. In the Name of Jesus…

"No thanks. I'm fine."

- "All you have to lose is your pain. Give me 10 seconds"

- "I know it may seem strange, but I believe God can heal you right now. (You might share a few brief testimonies… very brief, like I've seen so many backs healed, cancer, new joints) I know He'll do this for you. Just give me 10 seconds. All you have to lose is your pain."

- "I just want you well. I'm not out to preach to you or anything. I've seen God heal people and know He wants you well. He'll do it right now. So what do ya say? 10 seconds"

"But I am Muslim." (or some other faith system)

- With an enthusiastic smile, "Then you know that there is only one God and nothing is too difficult for Him. This is what I believe. He is good and great in mercy, right? So… Almighty God, thank you for this beautiful person. Thank you for healing. All pain, go now. Be healed. In Jesus Name!

There is no "method" that's going to open up every door. Rejection is part of the process of finding the people who are receptive. These aren't manipulation techniques. These are some lessons I've learned that will help you become more effective at connecting with more people for the sake of the Kingdom of God by avoiding unnecessary arguments. If you get rejected, resist the urge to evaluate yourself or criticize others if someone refuses to receive ministry for an obvious need. Keep yourself encouraged by keeping your eyes on Jesus and His love for others. Pray for the person who just rejected you (between you and God) even as they walk away. Whatever their physical condition, their rejection reveals an even more serious need and your prayers *will make a difference* in their lives for eternity. Continue to be thankful for the privilege of joining God on His mission to reach others and move on to the next person. Don't stop or slow down. As Jesus instructed His disciples, just shake off the dust and move to the next one.

*"Heal the sick in it and say to them, 'The Kingdom of God has come near to you.'
But **whenever** you enter a town and they do not receive you, go into its streets and say,
'Even the dust of your town that clings to our feet we wipe off against you. Nevertheless
know this, that the Kingdom of God has come near.'...***"The one who hears you
hears me, and the one who rejects you rejects me, and the one who
rejects me rejects him who sent me.***"* Luke 10:9-10, 16

One of the ways I've learned to handle rejection comes from Rom 10:20
which says, *"Then Isaiah is so bold as to say, "I have been found by those who did not
seek me; I have shown myself to those who did not ask for me."* So if people turn you
away, that doesn't stop your ministry. It just redirects your ministry. As you
walk away, you can declare over them, "Thank you Father that you will be
found by those who do not seek you. You will show yourself to those who
do not ask for you. So get 'em God! Show them your glory. Remove their
blindness. Capture their hearts!"

The way you handle rejection is as much a demonstration of the Kingdom
as preaching the gospel or healing the sick. One afternoon, I had taken my
family and some friends to a farmer's market. My oldest daughter, who was
about thirteen years old at the time, saw a lady with a four-pronged cane
who was sitting on a bench near the sidewalk. I watched her as she walked
over to the lady and said, "Hi! How are you today? I noticed that you were
sitting here with a cane and wondered if you have pain when you walk."
The lady responded, "Oh yes dear. I'm an old lady. When you get my age
you'll have pain when you walk too." To which my daughter smiled and
said, "No I won't. But I would sure like to pray for you. I've seen God heal
lots of people and I know that He loves you."

The lady immediately drew back and her countenance soured. She said,
"No thank you. I don't believe in God."

My daughter remained pleasant and undeterred. She said, "That's okay. It'll
still work because I believe."

At this point the lady stopped being polite. She said, "I said NO! Now
please let me alone."

So my daughter, continuing to smile peacefully waved goodbye and said, "Okay. I hope you have a great day!"

My daughter rejoined us and we walked on and prayed for some others.

About twenty minutes or so later, we were passing back by the same bench and that lady with the four-pronged cane spotted my daughter passing by. She got up off her bench and walked over to my daughter and said, "Hi there. I'm so glad I saw you again. I just wanted to say that it was very kind of you to take notice of me and offer to pray for me, and I had no cause to be rude to you. What you did was very kind and positive. So even though I don't believe, it surely won't hurt. So if you'd like to pray for me, I believe I'll take that prayer now."

Apparently, even though my daughter's initial interaction had not turned out the way we had hoped, the Holy Spirit had used the very act of approaching her in God's love to begin to deal with this lady's conscience. As we manifest God and deal with people in redemptive love, God's Kingdom will always be moved forward!

The best part was that as my daughter prayed for the lady, her hip pain decreased significantly immediately. My daughter introduced me (since I was with her) so we prayed together for the lady a second time and the hip pain was dramatically reduced yet again. Now the lady was standing there stunned with her mouth open in shock. So I told her, "Ma'am, I know there are a lot of mean and hypocritical people who claim to be Christians. But I want to let you know that Jesus Christ isn't like that. He's real. He's loving, kind and merciful, and everything He ever did He did for you. He wants to forgive you and heal you and be with you forever." At this point, she gave me a huge hug and began to weep on my shoulder... and all of this started with manifesting grace and redemptive love in the face of rudeness and rejection!

Healing the sick is one of the best ways to reach new people and open the door for the message of Jesus Christ. Everyone who has a body deals with pain and sickness. Healing is relevant to everyone. There are people who have no interest in hearing about God who become extremely interested once they experience the power of God's touch. Not only that, when people see that God works through you, they will begin to seek you out to connect you with other people that need God's touch in their lives.

While kindness and character are powerful demonstrations of the Kingdom of God, healing the sick is one of the primary demonstrations of God chosen by Him to accompany the gospel. Think about it. He could've given us all rods that would turn into snakes like Moses. He could make our eyes shoot laser light. He could allow us to levitate off the ground at will. But instead He's chosen to make Himself known through healing people. This is one of God's chief signs that accompanies the gospel. It's the music that fits the words of the song of heaven.

When people are healed from their sickness or set free from their pain, they are forced to find an explanation for what they just experienced. The ministry of Jesus in the gospels and the ministry of the church in the New Testament often follow this pattern. God demonstrates His power. Then the message of the Kingdom is proclaimed to explain what just happened. While miracles alone don't create saving faith, they create open doors for the message of the gospel. The gospel of Jesus Christ is the best and only true explanation there is. "He died to take away your sins, went to the whipping post to heal your body, and rose from the dead to give you eternal life. He's alive now. He's Lord and wants you to know that He loves you. He wants you to be with Him forever."

One of the driving forces in discipleship is learning to appropriate the power of God. When we are first hearing the gospel and being established, we are often receiving the ministry of God's power, healing our bodies, setting us free from demonic oppression, activating us in the baptism of the Holy Spirit with our heavenly prayer language, and giving us power to walk in victory over sin.

However, when the element of ministering to others in the power of God is added into the mix, some of the "deepest" truths of the New Covenant become self-evident *experiences, instead of just "positional truths."* When you add the power of God into discipleship, believers *experience*:

- "It's not I, but Christ dwelling in me"

- "By the grace of God I am what I am"

- "You will receive power to be My witnesses"

- "The old is gone, the New has come"

- "To as many who received Him, He gave the authority to be called a child of God"

When we disciple others by incorporating the demonstration of God's power in the gospel from the beginning, believers have the benefit of the experience that the Scriptures speak about. Otherwise, it's like trying to explain the color red to someone born blind, or the songs of a bird to someone born deaf. As Jesus said, "Unless you are born from above, you cannot *see* the Kingdom of Heaven." However, when we have the life of God active within us, we can indeed "***taste and see*** that the Lord is good." Once you've tasted God, you'll never hunger for anything else again!

CHAPTER 9

FREQUENTLY ASKED QUESTIONS

.

F.A.Q. #1

What about Timothy's stomach? Doesn't that prove that God was withdrawing the power to heal from the church towards the close of the writing of the New Testament?

"No longer drink only water, but use a little wine for the sake of your stomach and your frequent ailments." (1 Tim.5:23)

If you ever travel to a developing country, you'll be told "Don't drink the water!" Yet, when you arrive, you will see all the locals drinking the tap water. If you decide to go ahead and drink the water, it's very likely you will experience a battle over the health of your stomach even though your stomach is perfectly healthy. The locals are accustomed to the local microbes. You, on the other hand, are not.

Today we have bottled water. In the first century, they had a different solution. They would mix wine with the water to kill the microbes and make the water drinkable.

Apparently something had happened that had forced Timothy to stop using wine in the water. This was causing problems for Timothy's perfectly healthy stomach.

What was going on? From the context of 1 Timothy, we can make the following observations:

- Paul had to remove leadership from the church in Ephesus.

- Even though those leaders were no longer part of the church, they remained in near proximity and were still causing problems.

- Timothy was an outsider in a hostile situation. Timothy remained in Ephesus to raise up new leaders, which would make him the target of much negative scrutiny for anyone partial to the previous leaders.

- As Paul reviewed the standards for selecting elders and deacons, he specifically excluded people who didn't have the right practices regarding drinking wine.

Based on these observations, I believe that Timothy had decided to eliminate his use of wine in the water for fear of unjust criticism. Paul was aware of the pressure Timothy was facing and wanted to prevent people from using his standards of leadership against Timothy. For this reason, Paul specifically instructed Timothy to use wine for the sake of his stomach.

Paul's encouragement to Timothy to resume the use of wine for the sake of his stomach is not an indication that Paul didn't believe in divine healing for all or that there was some chronic problem with Timothy's stomach. Timothy's stomach was perfectly healthy. It indicates that divine healing is not in conflict with common-sense hygiene such as putting some wine in water, boiling water, or refusing to put your mouth on public water fountains.

F.A.Q. # 2

What about the people that Paul left sick? **Doesn't that show that even the apostle Paul didn't heal everyone?**

"I left Trophimus, who was ill, at Miletus." (2 Tim.4:20)

The Greek word translated "ill" in this passage is the word "astheneo," which is a general word that means "weak." It can refer to weakness because of sickness, but it can also refer to weakness for other reasons such as fatigue, exhaustion, and emotional pressure. It is a general word for weakness and does not equate to physical sickness.

We know from Scripture that the apostle Paul was a driven man with an aptitude for hard work and a high tolerance for conflict. It's likely that Trophimus found himself exhausted and in need of rest when Paul was ready to move on. Rather than wait for Trophimus to recuperate, Paul kept moving. This is a perfectly legitimate understanding of this passage that fits the context and the grammar.

But let's imagine that perhaps Trophimus is sick. It's time for Paul to leave and his trusted co-worker is not feeling well. He's in bad shape, is unable to eat and has fluids coming out of every possible opening. Paul lays hands, rebukes the sickness in the Name of Jesus, and hits the road without waiting around for Trophimus to fully recover. Does anything in that somehow indicate that Paul was unable to release the power of the Kingdom of God for healing?

Everyone I know who walks in the power of God today can share many testimonies of laying hands for healing with no immediate apparent change that resulted in an undeniable miracle in a short while. Just because Paul wasn't one to wait around, doesn't mean the power of God was no longer in operation in his ministry.

F.A.Q. #3

What about Paul's thorn in the flesh? **God wouldn't take Paul's sickness away, because he needed it to humble him. So I believe God is using my sickness to humble me.**

"So to keep me from becoming conceited because of the surpassing greatness of the revelations, a thorn was given me in the flesh, a messenger of Satan to harass me, to keep me from becoming conceited. Three times I pleaded with the Lord about this, that it should leave me. But he said to me, "My grace is sufficient for you, for my power is made perfect in weakness." Therefore I will boast all the more gladly of my weaknesses, so that the power of Christ may rest upon me." (2 Cor.12:7-9)

Many have made the assumption that Paul's thorn in the flesh was a sickness or disease. There is nothing to substantiate that interpretation and many reasons to believe that Paul was referring to Satanically inspired persecutors.

However, even IF (just for the sake of argument) we say that Paul had a sickness that was given to him to keep him humble, we must also look at the reason Paul said he received this thorn. Why did Paul receive this thorn? "***Because of the surpassing greatness of the revelations*** *there was given to me…*" Paul saw the resurrected and enthroned Jesus with his own eyes (Acts 9). He was personally discipled by the ascended Lord in the desert in Arabia (Gal. 1:16-17). He was taken into heaven and permitted to see and hear things that no mortal is allowed to speak (2 Cor. 12:2-4). He wrote two-thirds of the New Testament.

Good news! Until you write two-thirds of the New Testament, you don't even qualify for a thorn in the flesh. Paul's thorn doesn't apply to you. So let's get you healed!

Here's why I don't believe Paul's thorn was an illness: The phrase "thorn in the flesh" was a Biblical phrase that always referred to people who were persecuting the people of God (Num. 33:55, Josh. 23:13, Jdgs. 2:3). Furthermore, Paul says as much in the next phrase when he says that his thorn in the flesh is a "messenger of Satan." Jesus Christ bore our sins at the cross and our sickness and disease at the whipping post. But He didn't bear our trials or persecutions. We must bear those, and we can do so in the confidence that God's grace is always sufficient!

Regardless, if these poor people really do believe that I'm wrong and that they have "Paul's thorn" by way of a sickness or disease, shouldn't they just keep it? Why seek a medical cure for a "thorn from God?" The truth is, they aren't against getting rid of the thorn. They are just against having faith in God for miracles today. If it's really from God, stop being a hypocrite. Why not just keep it? Paul at least sought to get rid of his thorn through prayer. If they truly believe their sickness is equivalent to Paul's thorn, if the want to be Scriptural, shouldn't they be praying for a miracle and welcoming others to do the same?

Every Christian is free to follow their own convictions regarding the use of doctors and medicine in the treatment of illnesses. But in whatever we do, we must do in faith in God... not as an alternative course of action because you no longer have faith in God.

F.A.Q. # 4

Doesn't the book of Job prove that God sometimes allows sickness to serve a higher purpose?

Job wasn't in the New Covenant. He lived before even the Old Covenant. He didn't have the same provisions of grace or revelation that we have today in Christ.

The book of Job was in Jesus' Bible too, right? Yet Jesus never turned anyone who needed healing away saying, "I'm sorry I can't heal you. You are supposed to be just like Job and suffer a bit more." So let's fix our eyes on Jesus and walk in His faith.

The book of Job shows us that it is satan who afflicts, not God. Satan was seeking to demonstrate to God that he could turn Job away from God by affliction. God was using Job to teach satan a lesson (the righteous don't follow me for my blessings. They follow me for who I am in Myself!). God isn't telling Christians to embrace sickness as His plan. He's teaching us that none of satan's devices, even in the absence of any of His protection, can overcome us. However, now that the New Covenant has been established, we have received promises and salvation to a degree was not available to Job. In fact, Job prophesies that, if the resolution to his current misery would occur when his Redeemer, *"will stand upon the earth."* (Job. 19:25) Now that our Redeemer has stood upon the earth, we have the grace and protection made available to us that Job did not have.

In fact, when the book of James refers to Job's situation in the New Testament, it does so to encourage believers to pray in faith for healing, NOT to accept sickness.

"Behold, we consider those blessed who remained steadfast. **You have heard of the steadfastness of Job, and you have seen the purpose of the Lord, how the Lord is compassionate and merciful.** *But above all, my brothers, do not swear, either by heaven or by earth or by any other oath, but let your "yes" be yes and your "no" be no, so that you may not fall under condemnation. Is anyone among you suffering? Let him pray. Is anyone cheerful? Let him sing praise.* **Is anyone among you sick? Let him call for the elders of the church, and let them pray over him, anointing him with oil in the name of the Lord. And the prayer of faith will save the one who is sick, and the Lord will raise him up.**" (James 5:11-14)

God's purpose for Job was never His sickness or destruction. God's purpose for Job was his blessing. The book of Job is not intended to encourage us to remain sick. It's intended to show us that God wants us healed. It's satan who wants us sick.

F.A.Q. # 5

Doesn't it say that even Jesus wasn't able to heal people in his hometown because of their unbelief?

Many people have misunderstood the passages that describe one of Jesus' visits to his hometown. People imagine Jesus attempting to heal people with no results. So they reason, "If Jesus couldn't heal people in his hometown because of their unbelief, this must mean that the unbelief of others must be able to stop the operation of God's power, even for Jesus."

But this is a misunderstanding of what happened. Let's take a closer look.

"Coming to his hometown he taught them in their synagogue, so that they were astonished, and said, "*Where did this man get this wisdom and these mighty works? Is not this the carpenter's son? Where then did this man get all these things?" And they took offense at him…And he did not do many mighty works there, because of their unbelief.*" (Matt. 13:54-58-

Here's Mark's account:
"And he could do no mighty work there, except that he laid his hands on a few sick people and healed them. And he marveled because of their unbelief." (Mark 6:5-6)

When Jesus was in His home town, He healed everyone he laid his hands on. Yet "He was not able to do many mighty works." Why? Because they took offense and refused to allow Him to continue to demonstrate that He was the Messiah by healing the sick. They would rather allow the people they loved to remain sick, injured, and oppressed than to allow Jesus to continue to heal them since He had declared that His healing was demonstration that He was the Messiah.

"He cast out the spirits with a word and healed all who were sick." (Matt. 8:16)

Jesus hasn't changed. Let's walk as He walked and heal all who are sick. Amen!

F.A.Q. # 6

"Did I do something wrong that caused me to be sick?"

The enemy of our souls is a thief who loves to steal, kill, and destroy. Thieves don't care about rights. They take what they know doesn't belong to them.

Satan is also a deceiver known as the "accuser". After attacking people with sickness, he often tries to fortify his work against them with accusations of blame. He loves to whisper things like, "You should've done this…" or "If only you wouldn't have done this…" He knows that guilt can hinder us from laying hold of the fullness of God's provision for us because we doubt His favor.

This is nothing more than the voice of the stranger. The Lord is your shepherd and if you are His sheep, you know His voice. His voice builds you up in faith, in hope, and in love. His voice proclaims your favor and instills courage and joy. His voice equips you to grow into the fullness of the image of Jesus Christ. Don't follow the stranger's voice into a dead end road of regret and blame. Jesus *never* rebuked anyone for the illness of a loved one, or a sick person for their own illness.

God says those who need healing are "***oppressed by the devil***" (Acts 10:38).

Sin can give the devil an opportunity to attack. But it doesn't give the enemy a RIGHT to attack and oppress us. The devil lost his rights when Jesus Christ died and rose again. You've been set free from the power of darkness and transferred into the Kingdom of the Beloved Son. (Col. 1:13) The fact that you see better now only shows that God has given you a new heart. Now, stop wearing your old man and his deeds as your identity. Just go ahead and agree with your adversary on the way. Say, "You're right! I should have never done that. Jesus is Worthy!" Then rip the sword out of his hands and cut his own head off with it, saying, "God deserves perfect obedience. So Jesus Christ fulfilled the Law of God for me. I deserve death for my sin, so Jesus Christ died for me and I am crucified with Christ. God requires perfect righteousness, so I have called on the Name of the Lord and God has put Jesus Christ inside of me. He was made sin for me, and I have been made the righteousness of God!" Put on Christ and His righteousness. Rise up and look upon the blood of Christ with confidence. For it *"purifies our conscience from dead works to serve the living God."* Knowing that God is for you, not against you, take hold of all that you possess in Jesus Christ! Forget none of His benefits, who "forgives all of your iniquity, and heals all of your diseases." (Psalm 103:3)

F.A.Q. #7

Why can't you see this affliction as a divine blessing? Aren't you showing contempt for God's plan? Doesn't the Bible say that we will suffer?

Did Jesus Christ or the apostles ever rebuke anyone for not receiving sickness and disease as a divine blessing? Jesus Christ and the apostles always treated sickness and disease as a work of the enemy, never as a work of God, much less a blessing from God. If sickness is a blessing, then why did Jesus go around taking away people's blessings by healing them? If this is a blessing, perhaps you'd like to ask God to take away your health and give you these symptoms, or perhaps your child? May it never be!

The Word of God says that Jesus Christ went about healing all who were **"oppressed by the devil."** (Acts 10:38) The reason I don't see this as a "divine blessing" is because the Word of God calls it oppression by the devil.

The most common reason believers have a mindset of considering a disease a blessing is because they mistakenly assumed that all the verses about the spiritual benefits of trials and suffering indicate that God allows sickness in our lives for our spiritual benefit, but this is a mistake.

> Is anyone among you **suffering? Let him pray.** Is anyone cheerful? Let him sing praise. Is anyone among you **sick?** Let him call for the elders of the church, and let them pray over him, anointing him with oil in the name of the Lord. And **the prayer of faith will save the one who is sick, and the Lord will raise him up.**

Do you see the distinction? God wants those who are sick to seek healing, not just to bear up in the midst of it. But for trials we should persevere through them. For sickness we don't merely bear up under it. We should seek healing so that we can get rid of it! Jesus bore our sins at the cross and our sickness and diseases at the whipping post. He never bore our trials and persecutions. We must bear those. But we shouldn't bear our sins or sicknesses anymore because Jesus Christ already bore them.

As brother Curry Blake, General Overseer of John G. Lake Ministries, often says, "God is our help in times of trouble. He's not our trouble."

Jesus always encouraged faith for healing. He never accused anyone of resisting God's plan because they sought healing from a disease or affliction. The only people that genuinely "slapped God's face" were the religious hypocrites that arrested Jesus to hand Him over for crucifixion because they were offended that He would heal anyone, anywhere, at any time (including the Sabbath day). They preferred the security of their own theological convictions over the living God Himself. Jesus' word to them was, "Go and learn what this means, 'I desire mercy, not sacrifice.'" Some wise advice, don't you think?

F.A.Q. #8

I've believed all this for some time, but I've still not seen any change. Am I doing something wrong?"

When believers come to understand that Jesus Christ has already purchased their healing and given us authority to exercise dominion over the works of the devil (which include all forms of physical oppression), and yet remain in prolonged battle with illness, the question often arises, "What am I doing wrong?"

But if I were to ask you, "Have you stopped beating your children yet?" or "Have you stopped stealing money from your employer?", whether you answer "yes" or "no" you are going to be wrong. Why? Because the question itself is wrong. These questions have assumptions embedded in them— that you've been beating your children and stealing money from your employer and need to stop.

The question, "What am I doing wrong?" is packed with the assumption— "The reason that you are not healed is because you are doing something wrong." It's designed to get your eyes off of Jesus and onto yourself.

The more energy that you spend on analyzing yourself and your situation, the more you will lose momentum in attacking the enemy's works through faith. If the enemy can get you second guessing yourself, it will undermine your faith.

Faith is more than just agreeing that mountains can move or should move. Faith speaks to the mountain and it moves. Faith believes before it comes to pass, because *faith sees what is not seen.*

Many believers who are "speaking to their mountains" are also spending a lot of time allowing their mountains speak to them. Faith doesn't listen to mountains. Faith speaks to the Word of God to mountains.

Here are a few practical encouragements I suggest for believers who in a protracted battle with the enemy for healing:

1) Fix your eyes upon Jesus and saturate yourself with the Word of God. Only allow yourself to say what God's Word says. Take **every** thought and feeling captive.

2) Rejoice in the Lord always. Look beyond your situation and wrap your emotions around Jesus Christ and all His grace. If you are depressed or discouraged, this isn't coming from God. God isn't discouraged about you or your situation. Rejoice in Jesus Christ because the joy of the Lord is your strength.

3) Minister from the place of victory and joy instead of fear and need.

4) Even if you did somehow "do something wrong", you aren't trusting in yourself. You are believing in Jesus Christ who "forgives all your iniquity and heals all your diseases." (Ps. 103:3)

5) Get rid of your "miracle in a microwave" mindset, and get a "from now on!" mindset. One mother who had a child born with a serious birth defect told me about a conversation she had with her parents as she was explaining her faith for God to heal her child. Her parents asked her, "So how long are you going to do this?" (as if at some point down the road, if she doesn't see complete healing, it would be appropriate to reevaluate and/or give up). She replied, "I'm doing this from NOW ON! I'll destroy the works of the devil wherever, whenever, as long as I live, not just in my child, but everywhere in every person. It's not about us. It's about Jesus."

*"show the same earnestness to have the full assurance of hope until the end, so that you may not be sluggish, but imitators of those who through faith **and patience** inherit the promises." (Heb 6:12)*

F.A.Q. #9

I was told that my child's birth defect (or my condition) is a result of a generational curse. Is that true and if so what can I do about it?

The idea that people are walking around under the power of a curse that is passed down through the bloodline has gained a great deal of traction in the church. It is based upon a misunderstanding of what God spoke to Moses, when He said, *"You shall not bow down to them or serve them, for I the LORD your God am a jealous God, visiting the iniquity of the fathers on the children to the third and the fourth generation of those who hate me, but showing steadfast love to thousands of those who love me and keep my commandments."* (Ex. 20:5-6)

Since God said He will, *"visit the iniquity of the fathers on the children to the fourth generation of those who hate me"*, some have gone so far as to say that Christians should not adopt orphans, etc. After all, who wants to bring someone who is "cursed" into their home? Based on this same teaching, people have sometimes attributed genetic diseases and birth defects to a "generational curse."

However, a little careful observation of the Scriptures show that this is a terrible misunderstanding of this passage for several reasons:

First, there is no such thing as a "generational curse." There are "generational iniquities". There is a huge difference! A generational curse would be something like, "If you worship a false god, then your child will be cursed with birth defect" But that's not what God is saying. God is simply warning people who may consider turning away from Him that, apart from His covenant grace, He will not intervene to remove the impact of their sins upon their children. For example, if the father was a liar and thief, God was indicating that He would not intervene by stopping the influence of these iniquities on the lives of their children.

Second, God's warning of the impact of these generational iniquities was limited to those who 1) hate Him, and/or 2) bow down and serve other gods and 3) don't repent. Everyone gets to choose whether this verse applies to them. Will we love and obey God or hate God? The choice is ours to make.

Third, God's promise of loving-kindness, even under the Old Covenant, supersedes and overrules His warning about generational iniquities. Whereas God gives a warning that He will not remove the impact of the father's iniquities for those who hate him for four generations, He promises what is essentially unending steadfast love to those who love Him and keep His commands. So if ever anyone wanted to change the spiritual legacy that they were leaving to the generations that followed, they simply needed to repent. As soon as they repented, God's grace was now activated to overrule and supersede the influence of iniquity!

Forth, "generational curse" teaching is exposed as a false doctrine even in the Old Testament by the prophet Ezekiel. *"What do you mean by repeating this proverb concerning the land of Israel, 'The fathers have eaten sour grapes, and the children's teeth are set on edge'? As I live, declares the Lord GOD, this proverb shall no more be used by you in Israel… The soul who sins shall die. The son shall not suffer for the iniquity of the father, nor the father suffer for the iniquity of the son. The righteousness of the righteous shall be upon himself, and the wickedness of the wicked shall be upon himself."* (Eze 18:2-3, 20)

Lastly, through coming of Jesus Christ, we have the encouragement of even clearer revelation and a better covenant. Jesus specifically declared the sins of the parents were NOT the cause of birth defect in the man born blind. (John 9:3) Furthermore, His death on the cross has removed all the curses of the law from us. (Gal. 3:15) Through Jesus Christ, we are blessed with every spiritual blessing in the heavenly realms in Christ. (Eph. 1:3) Any curse that could possibly be in operation is cut off completely through the redeeming grace of the finished work of Christ. When you are born again, God becomes your Father and all He has to give you is spiritual blessings. You have the same spiritual inheritance as Jesus Christ!

So take courage, neither your child's birth defect nor any other affliction are a generational curse sent by God! They are an attack of the enemy, not the curse of God. They are resolved at the cross and the stripes on Jesus' back! Once you are a born again child of God, your body can partake of the healing in the name of Jesus. You can even give this power out to others in need, because Jesus Christ has blessed you with the power and authority to heal in His Name!

F.A.Q. #10

Why did God allow this birth defect? Is God punishing me or trying to teach me something?

If you are going to ask "Why did God allow this birth defect", you must also ask "Why did God allow you to be born a sinner"? God is no more responsible for a child being born with physical birth defect than for you being born a sinner. Both are a product of the fall and caused by the oppression of the devil, not God. God put Adam in charge on the earth. It was Adam who subjected the entire creation to evil when he bowed his knee to the devil. So it was Adam, not God, who handed himself and the entire human race over to satan and all his work. So it is Adam, not God, who allowed your child to be born with defect. It was God who sent Jesus Christ to rescue and heal us!

To look at a child born with defect and assume that God is responsible for the defect to God is a terrible misunderstanding of God. God created us in His own image and likeness to exercise dominion on the earth as we walk in union with Him. Any deviation from this is a result of evil, not God.

God didn't send your child's birth defect to teach you something. Even if you were a real stinker, God isn't going to afflict your child to teach you a lesson. He's not a Mafia boss that sends thugs after your children to get at you. God has sent the Holy Spirit to be our teacher. He is well able to guide us into ALL truth. (John 16:13) God doesn't need to enlist the oppression of satan to teach you anything.

I may tell my children, "Don't play in the park after dark because the older teenagers come out." If my son decides to stay in the park after street lights come on and gets his ball stolen and his face punched by some thugs, I may decide to take my son out for ice cream to cheer him up. We may have a special talk while we're out for ice cream that makes a lasting impression on my son. But my son would never dream of saying, "Dad I'm glad you sent those thugs to the park to teach me a lesson so I can get closer to you." Why wouldn't my son say such a thing to me? Because he knows me.

Jesus said, *"If you had known Me, you would have known my Father also."* (John 14:7) People who attribute sickness and disease to God need to reorient themselves to know the Father through Jesus Christ.

F.A.Q. #11

I know God can heal. I'm just not sure it's His Sovereign plan to heal me. I was told that if it's not God's sovereign plan for me to be healed, am I just being presumptuous. Am I being presumptuous to believe God will heal me?

Jesus shows us best how to acknowledge the sovereignty of God. He never treated sickness and disease like it was part of "God's sovereign plan" for anyone. Jesus always treated sickness and disease like it was a work of the enemy and represented rebellion against the sovereignty of God. The best way for us to acknowledge the sovereignty of God, which means His authority to reign, is to obey His commands and trust His promises.

Can you imagine standing before God on judgement day and saying, "The reason that I chose not to believe and obey what You said about healing the sick is because I wanted to acknowledge your sovereignty?" Does that even make sense? It makes far more sense to allow our King Jesus to be our sovereign Lord by following His commands which include "heal the sick".

Did Jesus ever rebuke someone who came to Him for healing by telling them they were being presumptuous? Or did He encourage us to come to Him for all the grace we need?

To show up at my friend's house without an invitation expecting to live at their expense because I assumed they would take care of me would be presumption. But to return to my parent's house for a holiday because they were encouraging and expecting my arrival and had already prepared a place for me is not presumption. It's trusting their love and taking them at their word. Hasn't God already paid for our healing and invited us to come and receive it through faith in Jesus Christ? Then how can it be presumption?

God commands His disciples to heal the sick. God sent Jesus Christ to the whipping post to purchase healing for our bodies. So if healing the sick is God's idea, how can I be acting in presumption? We didn't come up with the idea that God is our healer. This is how He has revealed Himself to us in the Bible.

God doesn't hold us accountable for reading His mind to discover a secret "sovereign plan" and acting only in accordance to it. He holds us accountable to be doers of the written Word of God. To fail to do what God commands and believe what God promises regarding His will to heal the sick simply because we insist on clinging to own theological views are far more presumptuous than simply doing what God tells us to do in His Word.

F.A.Q. #12

Sometimes I feel discouraged or depressed. I also have my own health issues. Can I still minister healing to others? Am I still qualified, or do I need to be well first?

Did Jesus make you discouraged? Or did you take your eyes of Christ and try to find your encouragement somewhere else? Never allow the enemy's work against you or others become the source of your identity.

The enemy tries to use our downfalls to cancel out the truth of the gospel in our minds. He'll whisper, "It is written that God always leads you in triumph in Christ, but you are still struggling with depression." You need to learn to cancel out your downfalls with the truth of the gospel. "I am still struggling with depression, BUT it is written, God always leads me in triumph in Christ Jesus!" The enemy will fight hard to keep you from getting settled in your identity in Christ, but you must learn to trust in the Word of God over your feelings and circumstances. We don't base our standing with God based on our walk with Jesus. Our standing with God was secured by the finished work of Jesus Christ. We walk with God based upon that, not the other way around!

Do people get healed just because you feel encouraged? Or do they get healed because of the stripes Jesus suffered on His back? If the fact that you feel encouraged won't heal anyone, why would you feeling discouraged stop anyone from getting healed?

Do people get healed just because you are in perfect health? Or do they get healed because of the stripes Jesus suffered on His back? If your perfect health won't heal anyone, how could your health issues stop anyone from getting healed?

You are qualified to minister healing to your child because of what Jesus Christ has done for you and them. Nothing can change that!

F.A.Q. #13

I've always believed that I will be healed in God's perfect timing. Isn't it true that if God wanted me healed, I would already be healed?

God is not up in heaven watching his day planner telling you to wait until next Thursday for your healing! Jesus Christ, in whom we see the Father perfectly revealed, was constantly being spontaneously asked to come and heal people. Never once did He respond, "I'm sorry, it's not God's timing just yet. Keep your disease until next Passover. When I'm back in Jerusalem, we'll see if it's God's timing then." Nor did Jesus ever say, "Why are you coming to me for healing? If God wanted you healed, you'd be healed by now!" No! Jesus demonstrated that God isn't waiting on right timing to do His works. He's waiting for a child of God who will act in faith so that He has a co-worker on earth through whom He can work!

God's timing for your child's healing was 2,000 years ago when Jesus Christ bore all our diseases and pains in His own body at the whipping post. He purchased complete healing for your child at a great cost to Himself. He has now entrusted you and I with the package He purchased— the Kingdom! You and I are simply receiving what Jesus has already purchased and released to us in the Holy Spirit.

What is God's perfect timing?

For he says, "In a favorable time I listened to you, and in a day of salvation I have helped you." **Behold, now is the favorable time; behold, now is the day of salvation.** *"* (2Co 6:2)

"Salvation" means far more than forgiveness of sins. It means deliverance from evil... all of it. "Salvation" means rescued, healed, made whole, and kept safe from all harm.

God's timing for salvation is always NOW. Our message is not that the Kingdom of God will come. Our message is that that the Kingdom of God is "at hand". God is not the great "I am going to be." He is "the great I AM." He is always present with the fullness of His salvation.

We don't say, "Who will ascend into heaven to bring it down." (Rom. 10:6) Yet many Christians act like everything we need is still up in heaven! Although it may sound like faith to call on God to send healing from heaven, the Bible says that is not how faith speaks! But there is good news! The veil has been torn! Just like water spills out all over the backyard when someone sticks a knife through the sides of one of those above ground vinyl swimming pools, the Holy Spirit and all the blessings that are in God Himself have been poured out into His people!

We proclaim that Jesus Christ is Lord NOW! He has all authority NOW! He is with us NOW! We are ambassadors of Christ NOW! We possess the Kingdom NOW! So we tell devil and all his works to go NOW because they are already defeated. The work of Christ is already finished so we declare it NOW!

F.A.Q. #14

My friends and family are telling me that I'm just avoiding the obvious, and that I'm not facing reality. What do I say?

Before you say anything to them, you need to allow the gospel to set your own heart free. You don't need to take other people's opinions to heart. There is no need to allow the opinions of others put you on the defensive. Let go of your idolatry of worshipping the affirmation of other people, and get settled and secure about who you are and your faith in Jesus Christ.

Once your heart is free, you will be able to respond in the way that is going to best allow you to pour out the love and truth of God to build up your family and friends. This is why it's so crucial for you to deal with your own heart first, otherwise you'll just pop off some "Biblically correct" response that is driven by your own insecurity.

Let your speech always be gracious, seasoned with salt, so that you may know how you ought to answer each person. Col 4:6

Here are some ideas for some possible responses:

- Share your testimony starting with, "There was a time in my life that I would've thought the same thing, but God changed my views. Let me share what I discovered…"

- If they are on the attack, just move off the subject, "Then you've badly misjudged me." You don't really owe people an answer. It's sometimes best just to remain silent, especially if you feel that they will just attack your answers.

Sometimes what is prompting people to accuse you of "denying reality" is because they don't see the same realities that you see. In some situations, you may be able to use this as an opportunity to share the gospel and preach the Kingdom. Make the devil pay! Every time someone brings up your situation, proclaim Christ! Get people saved and healed! The devil will soon begin to reconsider whether it makes sense to continue to try to keep you pinned down with this affliction!

You will likely find that some of the people to whom you are related or with whom you have been good friends are now genuinely opposed to your faith for healing and just trying to discourage you from believing God. You don't have to allow this to influence you. The light in you is far stronger than the darkness that is in them. However, as you are getting established in walking in the fullness of Jesus Christ, you should also seek out other like-minded people who can encourage you as you run your race.

God tells us to avoid people who deny His power. He warns that people will be "*treacherous, reckless, swollen with conceit, lovers of pleasure rather than lovers of God,* **having the appearance of godliness, but denying its power. Avoid such people.**" (2Ti 3:4-5) So if God tells you that there are some people you should avoid, you need to evaluate your relationships based on your current mission so that you can keep the focus on setting your child free. Don't feel bad for realigning your relationships to support your mission in the Kingdom. But often the best defense is a good offense! Be prepared to turn every mention of your situation into an opportunity to share the Lord and to speak of His glory!

F.A.Q. #15

I recently heard a preacher say that the reason we aren't experiencing a miracle is because we take medicine and go to the doctor. Is that right? Is it unbelief to take medicine or to give my children professional medical attention?

First, there are no pills big enough to stop God from healing you. If you or your children need medical attention, you are free to do it. There are no doctors large enough to stop God from healing. There are no commands in Scripture forbidding medical treatment. In fact, in many situations, doctors would be the first to admit that healing would require a miracle! You are free in Christ to believe God, grow up into Christ and to follow your own conscience regarding the use of medicine, doctors, and physical therapy.

If at any time your child requires medical treatment and you are not seeing supernatural healing, get your child the help they need. Don't make them suffer as the proving ground of your faith. God wants us well! One man once said, "If a man comes into your church with crutches, if you don't get them healed, at least don't take their crutches away from them!"

Some Christians who have embraced what God says about healing the sick have taken a very strong stand *against any use* of doctors and medical treatment. While believers are free to do this for themselves, when they impose their own views on everyone else, they are making the mistake of "teaching as doctrines the commandments of men" (Mt. 15:9) Jesus Christ sent His disciples out equipped to heal the sick with the supernatural power and authority of the Kingdom of God. Yet, He *never forbids* doctors and medical treatment for those who need it. In fact, although it's just an illustration, Jesus does say, *"Those who are well have no need of a physician, but those who are sick"* (Mt. 9:12) Furthermore, Jesus speaks of the good Samaritan commendably for stopping to give first aid treatment to a stranger and to pay for his ongoing care which likely would include medical care.

In all the Scriptures, I am aware of only one instance where God speaks negatively about someone seeking medical attention. In the case of Asa, God rebukes Asa for seeking the help of doctors, saying *"In the thirty-ninth year of his reign Asa was diseased in his feet, and his disease became severe. Yet even in his disease he did not seek the LORD, but sought help from physicians."* (2Ch 16:12) But careful reading of this passage reveals that Asa's problem was not primarily that he went to doctors, but **why** he went to the doctors. His heart was so hardened against God, he wouldn't even seek God when things were desperate. Asa was going to the doctors out of defiance because he was determined to prove he didn't need God.

As a believer in Jesus Christ, we trust God in all things. We are firm in our faith for complete healing and authority for supernatural miracles. As you walk this path, if you must go to the doctor, be like Hezekiah singing praises with his cake of figs. When Hezekiah was near death, he declared *"The Lord will save me!"* (Isaiah 38:20). Yet, in response to his prayer, God showed the prophet Isaiah *a medical treatment, "Let them take a cake of figs and apply it to the boil, that he may recover"* (Isaiah 38:21). It was an act of faith in God for Hezekiah to apply the cake of figs to his boils! Yet all the praise for healing goes to God and God alone! Notice also, that God commands a prophet to administer the medical treatment. So if it commendable for the prophet of God to give medical treatment, it must also be permissible to receive it.

In our ministry, we don't comment on anyone's use of medical treatment, doctors, or physical therapy. We make absolutely no recommendations. In the U.S.A. it is illegal for anyone who isn't properly licensed to do so. We keep our focus on Jesus Christ, not medical treatment or advice— that's for doctors. Jesus doesn't send his disciples out to distribute medicine or teach nutrition classes and exercise programs. We have been sent by Jesus Christ to release the Kingdom of God in miracles that will freak doctors out!

When it comes to seeking medical care (including doctors, surgery, or therapy) we encourage everyone to follow Jesus Christ according to the Word of God and according to their own conscience without feeling a need to defend their approach to everyone else. We live unto God, knowing that God has given the parents— not someone else, not the church or preacher, and not the doctor— the responsibility for their children.

If you are a parent, you must realize that you have the ultimate responsibility for the well-being of your children. But more than responsibility, you have the grace and power of God, who is the ultimate physician and able to do exceedingly abundantly beyond any doctor, according to the power that works within us!

F.A.Q. #16

My pastor is NOT on board with this. My pastor said that we must be very special to have been blessed with such a trial. This does not feel special. Is he correct?

Unfortunately pastors can get it wrong. As much as every pastor is doing their best to get it right, this is one area where many pastors have it wrong. The question for you is how should you respond?

Will you respond with offense in your heart born out of unmet expectations? Before you do anything concerning your pastor, I'd encourage you to first deal with your own heart. Sometimes we mistreat pastors because we relate to them based on expectations instead of the love of Christ and the revelation of their union with Christ. Let go of your expectations, disappointment, your need to be right, your desire for their approval and support, or any such thing. *"First get the beam out of your own eye, then you will see clearly to take the speck out of your brother's eye."* (Matt. 7:5)

Whenever I conduct one of my seminars, I tell people, "If you are here from another church, please don't go back with an attitude and start telling your pastor and everyone else that they are wrong. Go back and bear fruit. Take what you've learned and help people. Set people free. Encourage people. Build up others, not yourself!" We need to respect the fact that the leaders of the local church are doing their best to carry out their call to watch over the flock of God with integrity according to their understanding of God's Word.

Once you've allowed Holy Spirit to deal with any disappointment or offence in your own heart, you are in a much better place to consider your path forward.

Your pastor has the responsibility before God to help the church understand and demonstrate the Lordship of Jesus Christ, which includes the Lordship of Jesus Christ over all disease. If they are unable to provide proper spiritual leadership in this area, are they open to help? God has given you the assignment to act as His Kingdom agent to get your child healed. Is He asking you to help your pastor also?

Some pastors may be inspired by your faith and take the position of supporting you as you minister healing. In that case, you may want to offer this book as a resource to your pastor as a starting point to understand your approach to this matter.

However, some pastors would rather argue against your faith. You mustn't waste energy arguing with people, especially your pastor. You must press forward in the things of which you have become convinced even if you must stand alone!

You'll need to make decisions about what is the best way to find the spiritual leadership for the level of support that you need in this area of your lives. But your ultimate spiritual leadership and support will be Jesus Christ Himself and the comfort of the Holy Spirit.

Continue to sow to the Spirit and refuse to lose heart! In due time, you and your child will reap a mighty harvest for the Kingdom!

"Many will see and fear and put their trust in the Lord" (Psalm 40:3)

F.A.Q. #17

"Is it possible for me to minister healing, even though we are separated by a large distance?"

*"Truly, I say to you, if you have faith like a grain of mustard seed, you will say to this mountain, 'Move from here to there,' and it will move, and **nothing will be impossible for you."** (Matt. 17:20)

Jesus ministered healing at a distance in several instances, for example the Roman centurion's servant (Matt. 8:13).

If you are born again, the Lord Jesus Christ that is seated on the throne of heaven with all authority in heaven and on earth lives inside of you to accomplish His will through you. Christ has all authority in heaven and earth! So there is no place that His presence can't reach and act through your faith.

This can be done through the Spirit of God alone by faith. In our day, technology often makes it possible to have some remote contact, for example by phone or through the internet. I have ministered healing to all sorts of people through phone and seen many healings. My son holds the "long distance record" in the family though. We were ministering in a Chinese church and several of those who were attending used the skype app on their I-Pad. My son ministered to one older man who had terrible tooth and jaw pain that was healed instantly in China! That's a great way to use the internet, but I'm sure God can do the same things without an internet connection.

Another way you can minister remotely is through prayer cloths. This was done by the Apostle Paul (Acts 19:11-12). Just lay hands on the cloth and speak life into the object as if it were the person to whom you want to minister. Then send it to them. For children, cowboy hats, T-shirts, and stuffed animals make great "prayer cloths".

Instead of looking at the distance between yourself and your loved one as a disadvantage, you should realize this is actually an advantage! You have a greater opportunity to fix your eyes upon Jesus Christ without the interference that can sometimes take place when we "walk by sight". Because you don't have these medical conditions before your physical eyes, you can see them in spiritual perspective— as the work of defeated devils that has no hope of resisting the hand of an Almighty God! The works of the devil can no more stop God's healing work than darkness can keep light from taking over when it shines!

So fix your eyes upon Jesus Christ. Stand before the throne of grace to release grace to help and the power to heal as you walk in the confidence that God hears your voice and works through you!

F.A.Q. #18

"What will you do if you don't get healed? I have met many people who were hurt by theology like this. I am just trying to protect you."

I've met the kinds of people you are talking about. These are people who were hurt and offended because they feel like God let them down. They tried to reduce healing to a formula and leverage the Kingdom of God to make their own lives better instead of laying their lives down to know Him and become fully conformed to His image. They received the good news of the Kingdom, but when it was tested, they didn't have a firm foundation. Instead of seeking first the Kingdom of God and His righteousness, they sought healing merely out of their own self-interest. When it didn't work out on their timeline, they quit, took offense, and got bitter. You don't have to protect me from this.

How could I be hurt by a God who loved me enough to die for me when I had done nothing but offend Him? How could I be hurt by a God who always leads me in His victory? How could I be hurt by a God who found me as an orphan and adopted me as His own child? How could I be hurt by believing that God has revealed Himself as the one who heals, not the one who leaves us sick? How could I be hurt by a God whose own Son suffered merciless torture in His own body and soul to purchase healing for all?

If I am hurt at all, it is only by satan who continues to steal, kill and destroy; but not by Jesus Christ who came to give us life abundantly. It would hurt far more to embrace a theology that contradicted everything I see of God in Jesus Christ and call my heavenly Father the author and accomplice of this oppressive disease rather than the author of our salvation!

Jesus Christ has already suffered the stripes in His back for my healing. And I have received my healing. It's at work in my body right now. How could I be hurt except that I shrink back and begin to believe the philosophies and traditions of men over the very Word of God? Love never fails and doesn't seek its own, so how could I get hurt if I'm walking in love? "Faith pleases God" and "He who believes in Him will never be disappointed." You can't stop what's already happened. The only thing that I need protection from is living in the flesh and allowing mistrust, self-protection and double-mindedness to keep me from walking by faith in what God has already accomplished.

F.A.Q. #19

"Other people seem to be experiencing better ministry results than me. Am I doing something wrong? Is something wrong with me?"

There's nothing wrong with you. Jesus Christ purchased you, cleansed you, made you the righteousness of God, and dwells in you eternally. He removed everything that was wrong with you when He crucified you in His death upon the cross 2,000 years ago.

But you are definitely doing something wrong. You have misplaced your identity. You are comparing yourself with other people and getting your identity from what you don't see happening in your ministry instead of what has already happened in the body of Christ.

Here is something I have learned that may help you. Analyzing yourself and your situation is "the way of the old man." It's the carnal mind in operation, driven to figure things out and make life work to our best advantage because it knows nothing of eternal life. The "old man" is constantly analyzing itself because it believes that self-improvement is the key to everything.

The "way of the new man" is discernably different in the way it operates. Your new man knows you are a container of the living God. Your new man functions by faith, hope, and love in communion with God through our union with Jesus Christ. Is Jesus Christ sitting on the throne analyzing Himself saying, "Am I doing something wrong? Is something wrong with me?" Then He's not doing this inside of you either!

God is no respecter of persons. He's not playing favorites. So take encouragement from what you see God doing in one person's ministry is the same thing He will do through any of His children. What He does for one, He will do for all. Rejoice in everything you see God doing— no matter through whom it may come! Rejoice in everything you see in Christ! Throw off your self-interest and self-analysis and step back into your union with Christ and carry on advancing the Kingdom of God in faith, hope, and love, enjoying your fellowship with the Father.

F.A.Q. #20

I have a friend who isn't a believer.

Can they be healed?

Jesus commended faith whenever those who needed healing had faith. However, many times people were healed by someone else's faith. Jesus gives His authority to heal the sick, so we can heal the sick whether they have faith or not. As Jesus said, "Believers will lay hands on the sick and they shall recover." Mark 16:18. So a sick person doesn't need to be a believer. They just need to be sick and allow someone else to *believe for them* and lay hands so that they can recover.

One of the clearest examples of this is Acts 3, in which Peter and John healed a lame beggar on the way into the temple. The Scriptures say that, *"Peter directed his gaze at him, as did John, and said, "Look at us." And he fixed his attention on them, expecting to receive something from them. But Peter said, "I have no silver and gold, but what I do have I give to you. In the name of Jesus Christ of Nazareth, rise up and walk!"* (Acts 3:4-7) Was the lame man healed because he had faith for healing? Absolutely not! He wasn't in faith. If anything he was in greed. He wasn't expecting a healing. He was expecting money! Yet John and Peter were able to minister healing to this man. How? By their own faith in the Name of Jesus Christ, which is another way to say it was by their faith in the authority, power, and presence of Jesus Christ at work through them. We are to follow this same pattern.

I have seen this work out frequently in my own experience. In one instance, I was with a friend at Wal Mart. I approached a lady who was stocking shelves with canned goods with a smile and a nice "Hello!" She said, "Can I help you with something?" I said, "No, not really. But I think I can help you?"

She responded with a bit of curiosity, "Really? With what?" I replied, "Well, you are on your feet quite a bit, and I know that sometimes people are working in spite of their pain. Do you have anything giving you pain?" She said, "O yes. I have terrible knee pain. I'm supposed to get a knee replacement in a couple of weeks." I said, "Boy! That's expensive. I can help you with that. How would you like a knee replacement right now, for free!" She chuckled and said, "Yeah right! How are you going to do that?" I said, "It's easier for me to show you. And you don't even have to roll up your pants leg. Just hold my hand for a second." I held out my hand and she put her hand in mine cautiously saying, "O kaaaayyy." Then I said, "Just relax. I'm going to pray quickly and you'll be healed. Father, thank you for this precious lady. I Jesus Name, pain come out of the knee. Be healed right now!" Then I had her move around. She moved and her face fell. She began to squat and twist and stomp her foot. "This is incredible. It's all gone! My knee was killing me for months, now it's completely better." I said, "That's Jesus! He loves you." She said, "I don't even believe this." At this point she froze. Her face changed from puzzled excitement to fearfully protective. Then she said, "Thank you," and turned back to start shelving her tin cans. Her walls went back up… but now as she returned behind her wall, she stood with a new knee and the name of Jesus Christ ringing in her ears. I left her pleasantly to give her space and the Holy Spirit room to continue to work in her heart. Who's to say what the end result of this encounter will be for her.

But notice, this precious lady wasn't in faith when she got healed, nor even immediately afterward. She got healed because a believer laid hands on her, and she was healed. Jesus has given us that authority!

Appendix 1-

Seven Biblical Reasons

that Every Believer Should Heal the Sick

1) **Jesus sent many "non-apostles" out to heal the sick and cast out demons.** In Luke chapter 9, Jesus sent out the twelve to heal the sick, cast out demons, and preach the Kingdom. In Luke chapter 10, Jesus sent out seventy-two to do the exact same thing. So Jesus demonstrated that spiritual power and authority to heal the sick and preach the kingdom are NOT reserved for the apostles.

2) **Jesus commanded the apostles to teach us to obey everything He commanded them.** If Jesus Christ taught the apostles to "Heal the sick, raise the dead, cleanse lepers, cast out demons" (Mt. 10:8), then the apostles are under orders to teach us to obey those same commands.

3) **Jesus taught that miraculous works were for all believers.** *"Truly, truly, I say to you, whoever believes in me will also do the works that I do; and greater works than these will he do, because I am going to the Father."* (John 14:12) Jesus never tied miraculous works with the office of an apostle. Jesus said that walking in the miraculous was a "whosoever" thing, like "whosoever believes will not perish but have eternal life." Jesus expects these very same "whosoevers" who believe on Him for eternal life will "do the works that I do…and greater."

4) **Jesus is training ALL of His disciples to become like Him in EVERY way.**
Jesus said, "*A disciple is not above his teacher, but* **everyone** *when he is fully trained* **will be like his teacher.**" (Luke 6:40) If you are a disciple of Jesus, you are in training. Jesus has a goal, a vision for

your life as He trains you. He expects you to become just like Him. When Jesus was in the flesh to disciple the apostles, He trained them to heal the sick, cast out demons, and raise the dead. We are His disciples today. Now, in the Spirit He's training you to be able to do the same things... and more. He's not playing favorites.

5) **Jesus taught the apostles that miracles would follow "those who believe" the message they preach.** *"And these signs will accompany* **those who believe:** *in my name they will cast out demons; they will speak in new tongues; they will pick up serpents with their hands; and if they drink any deadly poison, it will not hurt them; they will lay their hands on the sick, and they will recover."* (Mark 16:17-18)

The signs of healing the sick, casting out demons, and supernatural protection from evil were not just following the apostles, but those who believe what the apostles preached. So, if you want these signs to follow you, set yourself to discover and believe the message that the apostles preached when they were sent out.

6) **Normal non-apostolic believers were used to do miraculous works in the New Testament.**

Here are a few obvious examples of regular believers being used for the miraculous:

Phillip, the Spirit-filled-food-distribution-manager

When the practical needs of the widows in the church became so labor intensive that the apostles needed some men they could put in charge of this task, Phillip was one of the people selected by the church. This allowed the apostles to focus on the ministry of the Word and prayer. So Phillip was obviously not an apostle, which meant that he shouldn't expect miracles in his ministry, right?

But when they believed Philip as he preached good news about the Kingdom of God and the name of Jesus Christ, they were baptized, both men and women. Even Simon himself believed, and after being baptized he continued with Philip. And seeing signs and great miracles performed, he was amazed. Acts 8:12-13

Apparently God never got the memo that He's not supposed to do miracles through blue-collar laymen.

The Scattered Tribes

The church started in Jerusalem with converts from Judaism who received Jesus Christ as their Messiah. The day Stephen was martyred, these believers began fleeing from Jerusalem. When James wrote to these "scattered tribes" of Jewish Christians, he addressed a variety of issues that the church was facing, including the way in which believers should respond to sickness.

Is anyone among you sick? Let him call for the elders of the church, and let them pray over him, anointing him with oil in the name of the Lord. And the prayer of faith will save the one who is sick, and the Lord will raise him up. And if he has committed sins, he will be forgiven. Therefore, confess your sins to one another and pray for one another, that you may be healed. The prayer of a righteous person has great power as it is working. Jms.5:14-16

James is giving instructions to the church for those needing physical healing for sickness. Does he say, "Call an apostle or you are out of luck?" No! He says, "Call for the elders of the church." The elders were not apostles, yet the believers are assured they would be able to minister healing when they pray the prayer of faith. But even in this case, the ministry of healing the sick was clearly not reserved for the elders of the church. Elders merely had a special responsibility to serve the church in this function, but every believer is encouraged to confess their sins and to pray for one another so "that you may be healed." Every believer was a potential minister of miraculous healing for the sick among the earliest scattered Jewish churches.

The Galatian Believers

"Does he who supplies the Spirit to you and works miracles among you do so by works of the law, or by hearing with faith?" (Gal. 3:5)

The apostle Paul is pulling out all the stops to rescue the churches in the region of Galatia from being taken captive to those who are trying to force believers to observe the Mosaic Law. So he points the church to their experience of the Holy Spirit. "How is the Spirit supplied? How does He work miracles?" Paul assumes that the believers in these churches are experiencing the miraculous power of the Holy Spirit and would be able to answer this question. He calls on their experience of God to bring up the answer, "You know Paul, you are right! When we experience the miraculous working of the Holy Spirit, it's not because we do a work of the Law. It's because we act in faith of the message of the gospel!" Paul knew that the message he preached had been believed and that the signs of a believer (casting out demons, dominion over the enemy's power, supernatural protection, and healing the sick) were following them.

The Corinthian Believers

To each is given the manifestation of the Spirit for the common good. For to one is given through the Spirit the utterance of wisdom, and to another the utterance of knowledge according to the same Spirit, to another faith by the same Spirit, to another gifts of healing by the one Spirit, to another the working of miracles, to another prophecy, to another the ability to distinguish between spirits, to another various kinds of tongues, to another the interpretation of tongues. All these are empowered by one and the same Spirit, who apportions to each one individually as he wills. 1 Cor.12:7-11

The apostle Paul was not trying to teach the church in Corinth about how to walk in the power of the Holy Spirit. He was teaching them about what they had already been experiencing, namely words of wisdom, words of knowledge, faith, gifts of healing, working of miracles, prophesy, discernment of spirits, tongues, and interpretation of tongues. This was not strange for the apostle Paul or for his churches. Paul expected that all his churches were experiencing the supernatural power of God at work in their midst without him or any other apostle present. To this apostle, normal Christianity was supernatural. The believers were experiencing the signs that follow the message of the Kingdom.

7) **Believers are taught to follow the examples and practices of the apostles.**
   "What you have learned and received and heard and seen in me—practice these things, and the God of peace will be with you." Phil. 4:9

The apostle Paul is teaching non-apostles to practice whatever they learned from him, heard him teach, and saw him do. Did Paul speak of miracles? Did Paul do miracles? So when the apostle Paul tells believers to do what he did and practice what he practiced, this would include the miraculous. We are to adopt a lifestyle of the miraculous with the expectation that God will also be with us as we do so. So, just in case you are not persuaded that miracles were not reserved for the apostles, in this command, every believer is told to do whatever they saw the apostles do. This includes miracles!

Additional Resources

You will find additional resources from Andy Hayner at his ministry website **FullSpeedImpact.com**.

The ***Born to Heal Interactive Training Manual*** is a powerful tool to learn the life-changing content of *Born to Heal* in small groups through direct interaction with the Scriptures. This is perfect to use even for those who have not read Born to Heal, or can be used for those who want to supplement and reinforce what they read in Born to Heal. It's designed with LifeTeams, small groups, and discipleship relationships in mind. You'll **learn for yourself** *through interactive, inductive Bible studies and life-changing practical activation exercises.* The perfect resource for raising up supernatural disciples of Jesus Christ!

Spirit Cry, by Andy Hayner, is a powerful devotional tool that will <u>accelerate your personal mind renewal and revolutionize your personal experience of God</u> by adding incredible depth, insight, and power to your personal fellowship with God. You will begin to learn how to use the Scriptures to speak to the Father as a Son and to hear the Father speak to you as a Son. If you are ready to learn how to use the Word of God to encounter the Spirit of God, get this book and get ready to unleash your Spirit Cry!

The book, **_Immersed into God_**, will equip you to experience your identity in Christ and to walk in His power to impact the world around you! Filled with examples, Biblical insights, and practical coaching, you will learn to experience God's power in your own life and to release His power to others by healing the sick, prophetic evangelism, and establishing disciples of Jesus Christ who walk in His supernatural power.

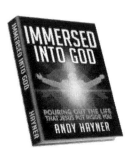

> *"This is an amazing book… There is so much packed into this book, that this will undoubtedly become a reference for years to come— for personal use, for cell groups, for churches, and for evangelism teams. Every new believer and seasoned leader will gain both Biblical answers and practical pointers to help release the Spirit of God to move through them at a greater level."* **Timothy Jorgensen**
> **author of _Spirit Life Training_**

The **_Immersed into God Interactive Training Manual_** is a powerful tool to learn the life-changing content of *Immersed into God* in small groups, LifeTeams, and personal discipleship relationships. You'll **learn for yourself** *through interactive, inductive Bible studies and life-changing practical activation exercises.* This is the perfect resource for raising up supernatural disciples of Jesus Christ!

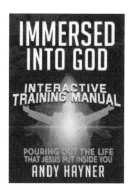

God Heals Birth Defects— First Fruits is a revolutionary book that will encourage, challenge, and equip you to minister healing in seemingly impossible situations. Written with a team of amazing parents from around the world, this book is packed with testimonies from parents who are seeing God heal their children who are afflicted with diagnosis such as autism, down syndrome, and cerebral palsy.

You will read of:

> ➢ Doctors amazed by disappearing defects
>
> ➢ Children moved to normal classes because they no longer qualify as "special needs"
>
> ➢ Organs, bones, facial features, and muscles restored to normal function
>
> ➢ Families restored to joy and peace by the truth of God's grace.

If you are looking for hope and practical Biblical answers that will empower you to minister healing to those afflicted with birth defects, and are ready to step into a lifestyle that truly manifests "All things are possible with God," this book is for you!

About the Author

Andy Hayner is a dynamic speaker and dedicated disciple maker with a passion to mobilize believers to walk in fullness of Jesus Christ worldwide. He is recognized for having a gift to impart a profound revelation of the believer's union with Jesus Christ in a simple, understandable way that unleashes greater depths of the love and power of God. Wherever Andy goes, the sick are healed, the lost are saved, and the saints are empowered to walk like Jesus. He has a passion for hands-on disciple making that has been developed through over twenty years of Christian service as a missionary, a pastor, and a church planter and Regional Director for John G. Lake Ministries, the oldest and most successful healing ministry in existence today. He is the founder of Full Speed Impact Ministries. He holds a Masters of Divinity from Columbia International University Graduate School of Missions. Andy remains a missionary at heart. He resides in Wisconsin with his wife and three children. You may direct ministry inquiries to FullSpeedAndy@gmail.com.

Made in the USA
Lexington, KY
28 April 2019